The Hemmings Motor News Book of

CADILLACS

ISBN 0-917808-54-1

Library of Congress Card Number: 00-106568

One of a series of Hemmings Motor News Collector-Car Books. Other books in the series include:
The Hemmings Motor News Book of Chrysler Performance Cars; The Hemmings Motor News Book of Corvettes;
The Hemmings Motor News Book of Mustangs; The Hemmings Motor News Book of Postwar Fords; The Hemmings
Motor News Book of Studebakers.

Hemmings Motor News
Collector Car Publications and Marketplaces
1-800-CAR-HERE (227-4373)
www.hemmings.com

Some words and brand names, for example model names, mentioned herein are the property of the trademark holder and are used by the publisher for identification purposes only.

The Hemmings Motor News Book of

CADILLACS

Editor-In-Chief
Terry Ehrich

Editor
Richard A. Lentinello

Designer
Nancy Bianco

Cover photo by Bud Juneau

This book compiles driveReports which have appeared in Hemmings Motor News's Special Interest Autos magazine (SIA) over the past 30 years. The editors at Hemmings Motor News express their gratitude to the following writers, photographers, and artists who made this book possible through their many fine contributions to Special Interest Autos magazine:

Arch Brown	Bud Juneau	Pat Tobin
Jeff Godshall	Michael Lamm	Russ von Sauers
David Gooley	Vince Manocchi	Josiah Work
Tim Howley	Jim Tanji	Nicky Wright
John F. Katz	John G. Tennyson	Vince Wright

We are also grateful to David Brownell, Michael Lamm, and Rich Taylor, the editors under whose guidance these driveReports were written and published. We thank Dave Holls, Strother MacMinn, and the Ramshead Collection, who have graciously contributed photographs to Special Interest Autos magazine and this book.

CONTENTS

Special Interest Autos (SIA) magazine's back issues are referred to in this book by issue number. If in stock, copies may be purchased directly from Hemmings Motor News at 800-227-4373 or at www.hemmings.com.

HARLEY EARL'S MASTERPIECE

1932 CADILLAC V-8

by Josiah Work
photographs by Vince Manocchi

I T has been said that of all the cars he designed during his long years as General Motors' chief stylist, Harley Earl's favorite was the 1932 Cadillac.

Small wonder. For in 1954 Earl would recall, "My primary purpose for 28 years has been to lengthen and lower the American automobile. Why? Because my sense of proportion tells me that oblongs are more attractive than squares."

Consider, now, how beautifully the 1932 Cadillac fulfills that objective. This was the last year, and the best, for Cadillac's "classic" look. It was the final season for the "tombstone" radiator, this time with the V-8 (or V-12, or V-16) emblem embedded in a fine square-grid grille. Long, sweeping "clamshell" fenders flowed smoothly into the running boards. Headlamps were sleek, bullet-shaped, glistening in chrome plating. The silhouette was lower than ever before, in part because the once-ubiquitous sill was omitted, partly because wheel size had been cut from 19 to 17 inches. Built-in trunks, supplied with the Town Sedan and the five-passenger Town Coupe, enhanced the appearance of length and served to predict the extended deck styling that would appear six years later on the Cadillac Sixty Special. And the new, slanted windshield gave just a hint of the streamlining that would be featured in later years.

Altogether, this car was, and remains, a styling masterpiece. It represents the culmination of an effort that commenced in 1925, when Lawrence P. Fisher, Cadillac's newly appointed general manager, summoned the young

Harley Earl from Cadillac distributor Don Lee's custom body shop in Los Angeles, and charged him with the design of Cadillac's forthcoming "companion" car, the LaSalle.

The assignment was supposed to have been a temporary one, but the short-term contract stretched into a lifetime career — one in which Harley Earl was to become, arguably, the most influential of all automotive stylists.

In the early years Cadillac had seemingly been disdainful of the whole matter of line and design. Old Henry Leland, genius of the firm's genesis, knew nothing whatever about styling and cared less. That tradition — if tradition is the proper term — continued at Cadillac long after Leland's departure in 1917. Not until the arrival of Larry Fisher, on May 1, 1925, was the car's appearance really taken seriously.

But if styling had taken a back seat, other factors had not. From the very

beginning Cadillac had been a quality product, marked by advanced engineering practices and built to exacting standards. Twice in the early years it had won the coveted Dewar Trophy, first in 1908 for its use of interchangeable parts and then in 1912 for its electric starting and lamps. And in September 1914 the Cadillac V-8 appeared, the first such engine to be offered by a volume producer.

It was a success from the very beginning. World War I came along precisely at that time, and although the United States was not yet directly involved, Cadillac was soon supplying ambulances for the Allies as well as limousines for the French General Staff. (Limousines? In wartime? Perhaps this helps explain some of the problems encountered by the French army during that war.)

Then there was the 1916 border skirmish between the United States Army and renegade forces commanded by Pancho Villa. Cadillac V-8 staff cars proved their mettle there, and went on to serve with the American Expeditionary Force after the United States declared war in 1917. Records from that time consistently praise the Cadillac for its durability, reliability and performance.

But the V-8 engine had one major drawback. Its crankshaft was similar to that of a four-cylinder engine, in that the throws were in a single plane, 180 degrees apart. As Maurice Hendry has explained, "This worked well except that there remained the secondary out-of-balance force normal in a four-cylinder engine." In the case of the 90-degree V-8, this produced a severe horizontal shaking force, particularly at the critical speed range of 40 to 50 miles an hour. No doubt about it, the six-cylinder engines featured by the competition — not to mention the great 12-cylinder Packard — were smoother!

The solution, which came in 1924 — more or less concurrently with Packard's new straight-eight — was a two-plane, fully balanced crankshaft. At last the Cadillac had smoothness to match its power. But because the V-8's cylinder banks were directly opposite one another it was necessary to use fork-and-blade connecting rods, which made the engine heavy, complicated and expensive to manufacture.

As time went along, further engineering advances made possible the development of a new generation of engines, in which the right cylinder bank was positioned an inch and three-eighths forward of the left. Plain rods could thus be fitted side-by-side on the crankshaft journals, resulting in a lighter, more compact engine — one that sacrificed nothing in either durability or performance, yet was much cheaper to build.

The new engine design was first introduced in the 1927 LaSalle, and then, in slightly enlarged form, extended to the Cadillac the following year. Eight-and-a-half percent greater in displacement than its predecessor, it was probably underrated at 90 horsepower, a 4.5-bhp increase from 1927. At least equally important, it also enjoyed the advantage of a shorter-stroke design. Specifically, the stroke/bore ratio for 1928 was 1.49:1, compared to 1.64:1 in the earlier unit.

There were other developments, as well. Four-wheel brakes were adopted in 1924. Balloon tires replaced the high-pressure type the following year. And with the introduction of the 1929 models in August 1928, the clash-free synchromesh transmission was featured throughout the line.

For 1930 the bore of the V-8 engine was increased by an eighth of an inch, raising the displacement from 341 to 353 cubic inches and the advertised horsepower to 95. But that wasn't the half of the Cadillac story that year. In an all-out effort to establish its supremacy over Packard in the hotly contested luxury field, Cadillac had undertaken what has been termed a "multi-cylinder" program. (The term is a misnomer, of course, since any engine with more than one jug is clearly "multi-cylindered." But let it go!)

The initial result of this undertaking, introduced in January 1930, was the Cadillac V-16. Powered by a spectacular 452-cubic-inch engine, it represented a departure from Cadillac tradition in the sense that it featured overhead valves with hydraulic silencers. (Cadillac V-8s,

our readers will recall, clung to the L-head design until 1949.) The 16-cylinder powerplant was awesome in appearance, smooth as cream in operation, and possessed of a very considerable thirst. But to the motorist who could afford the V-16's price, which ranged from $5,350 to $9,200 — more, if full custom coachwork was specified — the cost of fuel was a small matter.

Trouble was, the timing of the V-16's debut was atrocious, coming as it did less than three months after the Wall Street crash. To put the V-16's price in perspective, consider that in 1930 a brand new Chevrolet coach sold for $565; an Oldsmobile four-door sedan could be purchased for $995. Or to put the matter another way, for the price of the least expensive 16-cylinder Cadillac, the buyer could purchase a fleet of eight Chevrolet coaches together with a Pontiac sport coupe — and have five dollars left over.

Nor did the next step in the multi-

cylinder program help very much. This was the Cadillac V-12, introduced in September 1930 as a 1931 model. Another overhead-valve job, its prices started at $3,795 — enough to buy a rather nice little cottage in those days. Cadillac was not, to say the very least, in tune with current economic conditions.

The 12-cylinder series did prove to be rather more saleable, especially at first, than the 16, which really isn't saying very much. By 1932 the V-8, together with the lower-priced (but still very expensive) LaSalle, accounted for more than three-fourths of the division's sales. And five years later, 474 12-cylinder cars and 49 V-16s together accounted for just over one percent of Cadillac's total output. The multi-cylinder program doubtless served, to some degree at least, to enhance Cadillac's prestige. But as a commercial venture it was a failure.

It wasn't for want of trying. Prices on the 12- and 16-cylinder lines were cut

1932 CADILLAC

sharply for 1932. For that matter, the base V-8 sedan cost $800 less that year than the corresponding 1929 model. And certainly the prospective buyer was given a wide range of choices. Coachwork by Fleetwood was available in addition to the traditional (and somewhat less costly) Fisher bodies. In all, the division listed 62 distinct models, including seven LaSalles — with additional, full-custom styles available on special order. V-8 and V-12 models used wheelbases of 134 and 140 inches, depending on body style, while the gargantuan V-16s came on 143- and 149-inch chassis.

(By way of contrast, Chevrolet — with 40 times Cadillac's total output — catalogued just 14 models that year, all built on the same 109-inch wheelbase. Clearly, a considerable share of Cadillac buyers must have been expected to have their cars built to order, for no dealer could possibly hold all 62 models in stock.)

If Cadillac had a miserable year in 1932 (and it did, with sales running about one-seventh of their 1927 level), blame the economy, not the product. For the Cadillac line, in addition to being timelessly handsome, was improved in a number of respects. The V-8 engine, for instance, thanks to an increased com-

Above: For 1932 Cadillac's traditional round radiator badge grew curved wings. They lasted only for '32 and were replaced with straight wing design from '33 models onwards. Right: Cylinder designation was a supplemental badge carried on each model for '32. Below: Attractive trunk rack was a necessity on rumble seat-equipped cars. Bottom: Many Cadillac enthusiasts believe 1932 represents the pinnacle of that marque's styling excellence.

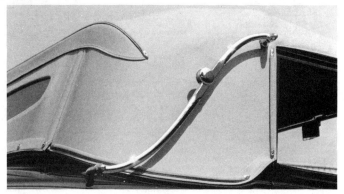

*Left: Even from this angle there's not an awkward line on the car. **Below left:** Flat windshield, thin pillars add to understated, elegant look. **Below:** As do the graceful landau bars.*

Driving Impressions

Nowadays, as the Lincoln commercials are careful to remind us, it isn't always easy to distinguish a Cadillac from a Buick Park Avenue or an Olds Ninety-Eight. Styling is similar; size and weight are virtually identical; performance and handling aren't all that different. Even the price doesn't represent very much of a spread.

It wasn't always so. Back in 1932, when our driveReport car was built, a Cadillac convertible cost three times as much as an Oldsmobile ragtop. It was 25½ inches longer and 61 percent heavier than the car from Lansing, though the power-to-weight ratio of the two cars was nearly identical.

It's the weight, of course, that makes the big difference in how the Cadillac handles and performs. That and its size, which is enormous by 1932 standards. And that's the first thing we noticed in driving this automobile. It is ponderous! It's at its best on the open road, where it will cruise quietly and happily at 65 miles an hour, with bursts up to nearly 90 if anyone is insane enough to push it that hard. Or so we're told; we didn't try anything so foolhardy. But in city traffic the Cadillac won't win any awards for agility.

So this is not, by anyone's definition, a high-performance automobile. It's built for comfort, and despite its impressive top speed we found the acceleration to be no better than adequate. The vacuum-assisted double-plate clutch is light and smooth. And the synchro-mesh transmission, fitted with constant-mesh helical gears for silent operation, is a joy to use. Steering, as one might expect, is extremely heavy until the car gathers speed. Once under way, the big convertible can be guided with only moderate effort, but parking is really a chore. And the 44-foot turning diameter does little to

facilitate U-turns.

We've always distrusted "free-wheeling," but the Cadillac's arrangement — shared with Buick — is better than most. Operated by means of a button located under the clutch pedal, it is basically a vacuum-operated clutch designed to disengage drive on demand, thus permitting the driver to shift gears without the use of the conventional clutch.

"Suicide" doors give easy access to the passenger compartment, and the seats are exceptionally comfortable and supportive. Some degree of adjustment is provided on the driver's side, but leg room is marginal for a six-footer, and the short person is well-advised to bring along a pillow. The ride, not unexpectedly, is luxurious — though it can't match that of the later Cadillacs with their independent front suspension.

An interesting device is the "Ride Regulator," which enables the driver to adjust the action of the hydraulic shock absorbers to provide five distinct degrees of firmness or softness. Thus the car's ride can be matched to its load, to road conditions, or to the driver's individual preferences.

Cadillac was not quick to recognize the advantages of hydraulic brakes. Not until 1936 did the division finally adopt that feature for its senior cars, though its lower-priced companion marque, the LaSalle, used juice brakes as early as 1934. We found the mechanical binders to be satisfactory as fitted to the 4,675-pound V-8 convertible. But the same brakes — aided, to be sure, by a vacuum booster — were employed on 12-cylinder limousines weighing as much as 5,580 pounds, and we question whether they're really adequate for that kind of duty.

Having said that, we hasten to add that

we found this Cadillac to be an automobile that truly inspires respect. It's a solid, durable machine, of superb quality in every respect. And it's certainly a stylish and comfortable one. It has a number of little features that we like, too, such as the golf club door with its automatic light; the full set of handsome, legible instruments; the gorgeous (and impressive-sounding) trumpet horns.

This particular car has had an incredible history, for in 1983 it was literally dug out of a Southern California chicken coop. Taken by its owners, Charles and Sarah Chastain, to Paul Batista's excellent restoration facility in Ontario, California, it was torn down to the frame and completely rebuilt. "It was an absolute mess," Batista recalls. One side of the engine block was cracked, as was one cylinder head. The wood framing of the body was rotted; it had to be completely replaced. (Incidentally, contrary to a commonly held opinion, oak is not the preferred wood for this purpose. In this instance poplar and pecan were employed.) Every single component was meticulously renewed or replaced, and finishing touches were applied in the form of red leather upholstery, a tan Hartz canvas top and fresh lacquer in Deep Viceroy Maroon with vermilion striping and wheels — an authentic 1932 Cadillac color scheme.

Altogether it was a major undertaking. But from a pile of junk in a farmer's chicken coop the Cadillac was transformed — like Cinderella — into an award-winning beauty: First in Class at Hershey, 1986, and Best of Show at the Ascot Invitational that same season. Then, in 1987, the ultimate accolade for a car: a first place in class at the Pebble Beach Concours d'Elegance. And you can't do better than that!

specifications

Illustrations by Russell von Sauers, The Graphic Automobile Studio

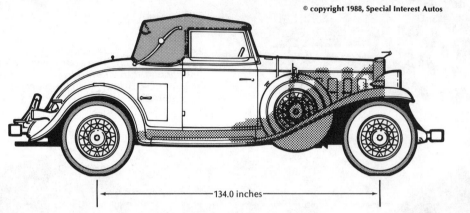
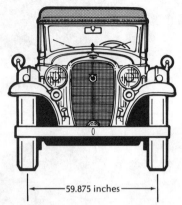

← 134.0 inches →   ← 59.875 inches →

1932 Cadillac V-8 Convertible Coupe

Price	$2,945, f.o.b factory (with standard equipment)
Options on dR car	Radio, heater, twin sidemounts, metal tire covers, twin outside mirrors, white sidewall tires, trunk rack, Cadillac goddess radiator ornament.

ENGINE

Type	90° V-8, cylinder banks separately cast
Bore x stroke	3⅜ inches x 4 15/16 inches
Displacement	353.4 cubic inches
Max bhp @ rpm	115 @ 3,000
Max torque @ rpm	n/a
Taxable hp	36.45
Compression ratio	5.38:1
Valves	L-head
Valve lifters	Solid
Main bearings	3
Lubrication system	Pressure
Induction system	2-inch dual updraft carburetor, camshaft pump
Exhaust system	Single
Electrical system	6-volt
Cooling system	Centrifugal pump

CLUTCH

Type	Multiple dry disc
Diameter	10 inches
Actuation	Foot pedal with vacuum assist; free-wheeling unit

TRANSMISSION

Type	3-speed selective, synchronized 2nd and 3rd gears
Ratios: 1st	2.40:1
2nd	1.47:1
3rd	1.00:1
Reverse	2.49:1

DIFFERENTIAL

Type	Spiral bevel
Ratio	4.36:1
Drive axles	¾ floating
Torque medium	Torque tube

STEERING

Type	Worm and sector
Ratio	17:1
Turn circle	44 feet, 0 inches

BRAKES

Type	Internal 4-wheel mechanical
Drum diameter	12 inches
Effective area	238 square inches

CHASSIS & BODY

Type	Body on frame
Frame	Double drop with box-type cross members
Body construction	Composite, steel over wood framing
Body style	2-4 passenger convertible coupe

SUSPENSION

Front	I-beam axle, 39-inch x 2¼-inch semi-elliptic springs
Rear	Conventional axle, 58-inch x 2¼-inch semi-elliptic springs
Wheels	Welded steel spoke
Tires	7.00/17

WEIGHTS AND MEASURES

Wheelbase	134 inches
Overall length	204 inches
Overall width	77 inches
Overall height	71 inches
Front track	59⅞ inches
Rear track	61 inches
Ground clearance	7⅝ inches minimum
Shipping weight	4,675 pounds

CAPACITIES

Crankcase	8 quarts
Transmission	4½ pounds
Cooling system	26 quarts
Fuel tank	30 gallons

CALCULATED DATA

HP/c.i.d.	.325
Pounds/hp	40.7
Pounds/c.i.d.	13.2
Pounds/sq. in. (brakes)	19.6

This page: You can see where the '32 Chevrolets derived their good looks. *Facing page, above left:* Parking lamps were exact miniatures of the headlamps. *Above right:* Sidemount mirrors are intricately inscribed and carry Cadillac crest. *Below left:* Instrument panel is clear to read and pleasingly symmetrical. *Below right:* Pair of big chromed horns adds to impressive frontal treatment.

1932 CADILLAC

pression ratio and certain other modifications, was boosted from 95 to 115 horsepower, an increase of 21 percent. Helical gears virtually eliminated transmission noise in all forward speeds. And a Ride-Regulator enabled the driver to adjust the action of the shock absorbers to suit road conditions and the load to be carried.

But all this was to no avail. Cadillac's

Cadillac Meets The Competition: A Comparison Table

	Cadillac V-8	LaSalle V-8	Chrysler Imp. Cust.	Packard Std. 8	Pierce-Arrow 54	Reo Royale Custom	Buick 90	Nash 1090	Studebaker State President
Price, convertible coupe	$2,945	$2,545	$3,295	$2,850	$3,100	$2,995	$1,805	$1,795	$1,855
Wheelbase	134″	130″	146″	137″	137″	135″	134″	133″	135″
Weight (pounds)	4,675	4,630	5,065	4,525	4,650	4,440	4,660	4,270	4,200
Engine c.i.d.	353.4	353.4	384.8	319.2	365.6	357.8	344.8	322.1	336.7
Horsepower/rpm	115/3,000	115/3,000	125/3,200	110/3,200	125/3,000	125/3,300	113/3,200	125/3,600	122/3,200
Compression ratio	5.38:1	5.38:1	5.20:1	6.00:1	5.05:1	5.30:1	4.80:1	5.25:1	5.10:1
Valve configuration	L-head	L-head	L-head	L-head	L-head	L-head	OHV	OHV	L-head
Main bearings	3	3	9	9	9	9	5	9	9
Axle ratio	4.36:1	4.36:1	3.82:1	4.69:1	4.08:1	3.77:1	4.27:1	4.50:1	4.31:1
Brakes	Mech	Mech	Hydr	Mech	Mech	Hydr	Mech	Mech	Mech
HP/c.i.d.	.325	.325	.325	.345	.342	.349	.328	.388	.362
Lbs/HP	40.7	40.3	40.5	41.6	37.2	35.5	41.2	34.2	34.4

(Note how close some of the upper-medium-priced cars came to matching the luxury machines in terms of size and horsepower, at a cost savings of something over a thousand dollars. Also note that the power-to-weight ratio of the Studebaker and the Nash would suggest that these cars should be capable of out-performing our driveReport Cadillac. The sad fact is, however, that in the Depression market, none of the cars listed sold very well.)

Above: 353-cubic-inch flathead V-8 was Cadillac mainstay until new 346 V-8 appeared for 1936. *Below left:* Driving compartment is understated and luxurious. *Below right:* Now you know the inspiration for all those accessory "blue dot" taillamps!

MAY | CALIFORNIA | CA 87
CAD 355B

Above: Sidemount tires tuck low into fenders for sporty appearance.

1932 CADILLAC

1932 calendar year production was at the lowest level since 1914, the final year of the four-cylinder Cadillac. The situation would improve just slightly in 1933, and a further gain would be made in 1934, thanks to a new, relatively inexpensive LaSalle. But not until Cadillac undertook to open up a new, more moderately priced market with the Series 60 in 1936 (see *SIA* #69) would the division be restored to anything approaching its pre-Depression volume.

Styling, under Harley Earl's leadership, evolved gradually. The 1933 models represented a transitional step, combining a vee'd radiator grille and skirted fenders with the more traditional lines of the 1932 body shell. Increasingly, thereafter, streamlining became the order of the day, and if the 1934-35 Cadillacs look a little awkward today, they can at least be credited with paving the way for Bill Mitchell's gorgeous 1938 Sixty-Special (see *SIA* #62).

Our driveReport car, then, represents virtually the last of the traditionally styled Cadillacs, a reminder of a past that was as magnificent in concept as it was disastrous on the sales floor. It represents a time that none of us would care to repeat, a time of bread lines and apple vendors, of bankruptcies and foreclosures, a time of little hope. Yet it also represents, from an artist's perspective, the pinnacle of automotive design. ⚙

Acknowledgments and Bibliography

Automobile Trade Journal (*various issues*); Automotive Industries (*various issues*); James D. Bell, "The Cadillac

Price List: 1932 Cadillac and LaSalle

	LaSalle	Cadillac 8	Cadillac 12	Cadillac 16
Fisher Bodies				
Roadster		$2,895	$3,595	$4,595
Coupe	$2,395	$2,795	$3,495	$4,495
Sedan	$2,495	$2,895	$3,595	$4,595
Convertible Coupe	$2,545	$2,945	$3,645	$4,645
Phaeton		$2,995	$3,695	$4,695
Special Phaeton		$3,095	$3,795	$4,795
Sport Phaeton		$3,245	$3,945	$4,945
All-Weather Phaeton		$3,495	$4,195	$5,195
Coupe, 5-passenger	$2,545	$2,995	$3,695	
Special Sedan		$3,045	$3,745	
Town Sedan	$2,645	$3,095	$3,795	
Sedan, 7-passenger	$2,645	$3,145	$3,845	
Imperial Sedan	$2,795	$3,295	$3,995	
Fleetwood Bodies				
Sedan		$3,395	$4,095	$5,095
Town Coupe		$3,395	$4,095	$5,095
Sedan, 7-passenger		$3,545	$4,245	$5,245
Limousine		$3,745	$4,445	$5,445
Town Cabriolet		$4,095	$4,795	$5,795
Town Cabriolet, 7-pass.		$4,245	$4,945	$5,945
Limo, Brougham		$4,245	$4,945	$5,945
Model Year Production	3,386	2,693	1,709	296
Total Model Year Production (all series, including LaSalle): 8,084				
Total Calendar Year Production (all series, including LaSalle): 9,153				
Sources: Automobile Trade Journal, August 1932. Jerry Heasley, The Production Figure Book fo US Cars				

Above: Wire wheels were standard equipment.

Standard," Automobile Quarterly, *Volume III, Number 3*; Cadillac factory literature; *Richard Burns Carson,* The Olympian Cars; *Jerry Heasley,* The Production Figure Book for US Cars; *Maurice D. Hendry,* Cadillac: The Complete History; *Richard M. Langworth and Jan P. Norbye,* The Complete History of General Motors; *Walter M.P. McCall,* Eighty Years of Cadillac-LaSalle; *Alfred P. Sloan, Jr.,* My Years With General Motors.

Our thanks to Paul Batista, Batista-Chastain Restorations, Ontario, California; Ray Borges, William F. Harrah Automobile Foundation, Reno, Nevada; Dave Brown, Durham, California; Vince Manocchi, Azusa, California. Special thanks to Charles and Sarah Chastain, Bell Canyon, California.

Top right: Proud restorer Paul Batista before Cadillac won prize at Pebble Beach Concours. *Above left:* No proper high-priced sportster would be without a golf club door. *Above right:* Rumble seat offers plenty of room once you've crawled inside.

1932

It was, to paraphrase Charles Dickens, the worst of times. E.Y. "Yip" Harburg said it all, in the words of a popular song of the day:

They used to tell me I was building a dream
With peace and glory ahead.
Why should I be standing in line
Just waiting for bread?

Once I built a tower to the sun,
Brick and rivet and lime.
Once I built a tower, now it's done.
Brother, can you spare a dime?

President Herbert Hoover confidently predicted that prosperity was "just around the corner." Perhaps Roy Chapin believed him, for he left his job as chairman of the board at the Hudson Motor Car Company to become Secretary of Commerce in the closing months of the Hoover administration.

Nostrums were applied, but nothing helped. Wall Street was in total disarray. Unemployment was at an all-time high, while wages were in precisely the opposite position. Unskilled jobs sometimes paid as little as 15 cents an hour—and men were glad to get them, even at that pittance! It's difficult to imagine, 56 years later, just how desperate conditions had become.

People sought to forget. They flocked to the movies: 25 cents bought a ticket to a double bill at the neighborhood theater. Perhaps a first-run show at one of the art deco palaces downtown might cost as much as 40 cents. There, one could see Greta Garbo and the brothers Barrymore in "Grand Hotel"; Fredric March as "Dr. Jekyll and Mr. Hyde"; Ronald Coleman and Helen Hayes in Sinclair Lewis's "Arrowsmith." And a pair of talented young dancers, Fred Astaire and Ginger Rogers, were a smash hit in a sparkling Cole Porter musical called "The Gay Divorcee."

Nobody seems to remember a Broadway show named "Walk a Little Faster," which opened on December 7, 1932. But the hit song from that production, "April in Paris," has become immortal. A young crooner named Bing Crosby was making it big with songs such as "I Surrender Dear." Duke Ellington, just leaving Harlem's Cotton Club after a five-year engagement, enhanced his rising reputation with "It Don't Mean a Thing If It Ain't Got That Swing." And Britain's Ray Noble enchanted American listeners with the likes of "Love Is The Sweetest Thing."

Aviatrix Amelia Earhart became the first woman to fly solo across the Atlantic, touching down in Londonderry, Ireland, on May 21, 1932. It cost eight cents—four times the normal rate—if one chose to send a letter by airmail in those days. And the infant son of Charles A. Lindbergh—America's national hero, then—was kidnapped and murdered.

Dashiell Hammet introduced *The Thin Man* to the world of literature that year. Erskine Caldwell achieved immortality with *Tobacco Road,* and John Dos Passos chronicled *Mark Twain's America. Grover Cleveland,* a biography by Allan Nevins, and Archibald MacLeish's epic poem, *Conquistador,* were on their way to winning Pulitzer prizes. And Thorne Smith's *The Bishop's Jaegers* provided a welcome bit of hilarity.

Detroit, meanwhile, was a disaster area. Durant and Peerless closed up shop early in the season. Gardner, Jordan, and Moon had folded the year before. Marmon and Stutz would follow shortly, and Hupmobile and Graham were fading. Only General Motors and Nash made money that year. Not much of it, to be sure, but how they managed to eke out any profit at all remains a mystery. For GM's sales were off by 71.3 percent compared to their 1928 total, and Nash had tumbled by an astonishing 87.2 percent over the same four-year period.

Given such a state of affairs, it is easy enough to picture the plight of the hapless Cadillac salesman. Few could afford a new car in those troubled times. Any new car, much less a machine that cost three times as much as a Series 50 Buick! and even those few who had somehow managed to retain some semblance of solvency would surely have been hesitant to flaunt their wealth at a time when people were literally going hungry.

And so, only 4,698 Cadillacs left the factory during the 1932 model year. How many of those were V-8 convertible coupes like our driveReport car, nobody knows for sure. Not many, you may be certain, for people tended to regard a convertible as frivolous. And 1932 was not the time for frivolity.

REGAL RAGTOP

1935 CADILLAC V-12
FLEETWOOD CONVERTIBLE SEDAN

by Arch Brown
photos by Bud Juneau

O N July 30, 1930, Cadillac general manager Lawrence P. Fisher announced to a group of his distributors that a V-12 was being prepared for introduction that October, in order to compete head-to-head with 12-cylinder models from Lincoln, Pierce-Arrow and Packard. Especially Packard, the leading marque in the high-priced field in those days.

One could almost think of Cadillac's V-12 as an afterthought, for it was clearly based upon the V-16 that had been introduced the previous January. Richard Burns Carson has described the 12-cylinder engine as a "368-cubic-inch version of the V-16 with the four center cylinders eliminated." Which is just what it was, except that the bore had been increased from three inches to three and one eighth inches, yielding a displacement of 353.4 cubic inches.

Anxious that the 16-cylinder engine should be the smoothest powerplant available anywhere, Cadillac had designed it with a 45-degree angle between the cylinder

Originally published in Special Interest Autos #133, Jan.-Feb. 1993 banks, thus assuring an absolutely even firing order. Had the V-12 been designed from scratch, presumably the angle would have been 60 degrees, in order to achieve the same effect. But the truth of the matter is, when there are 12 cylinders firing, and the crankshaft is counterbalanced and a vibration damper is employed, any irregularity in the firing impulses is so effectively masked as to be almost imperceptible. No one has ever described the Cadillac V-12 engine as anything but smooth.

In fact, among the several V-12s produced by US automakers during the early and mid-thirties, only Franklin placed its cylinder banks at a 60-degree angle from one another – the theoretical ideal. Packard and Lincoln came close, employing a 67-degree vee, while Pierce-Arrow used an unusual 80 degrees. Auburn, like Cadillac, featured a 45-degree placement, which confirms what Pat Tobin told us in *SIA #119*, that the Auburn V-12 was developed from a 16-cylinder prototype.

Cadillac had been building highly successful V-8s since 1915, all using the L-head configuration. But in a departure from company tradition, the 12- and 16-cylinder models employed overhead valves. This design was evidently selected in the interest of accessibility, given the unusually narrow angle between the cylinder banks, but as Maurice Hendry has observed in his book, *Cadillac, The Complete History*, the ohv design "appear[s] to have given some gain in specific output." The figures seem to bear this out, for the Cadillac V-12, while much smaller in displacement than its side-valve competitors, produced substantially more horsepower per cubic inch than any of them (see sidebar, page 17). Given this experience, we're at a loss to explain why Cadillac waited until 1949 to adopt overhead valves for its eight-cylinder engines.

One occasionally runs across the assertion that the Cadillac V-12 would out-perform the V-16. If true, this would be remarkable, for the twelve carried five and a half more pounds per horsepower than the sixteen. And according to Hendry, "GM Proving Ground data reveal the V-16 to be seven miles an hour faster than the V-12."

The 12-cylinder Cadillac came to market as a 1931 model, and 5,725 examples were produced that season. Not a bad start, given the state of the nation's economy at the time, but it's a safe bet that the V-12 stole a substantial number of its sales from the more profitable V-16. After all, the 12-cylinder, five-passenger sedan sold for $3,895, a cool $2,055 less than the sixteen in the same body style. Think of it this way: For the price of that V-16 sedan, the buyer could have had a V-12

Above: "Flipper" style wheel covers first appeared on 1933 sixteen-cylinder cars. Below: Only external clue to engine size appears at leading edge of hood louvers.

with enough left over to finance the purchase of both a Buick 50 convertible and an Oldsmobile Patrician sedan.

Critics generally agree that the 1932 models were among the most beautiful Cadillacs ever built. In an effort to stimulate sales, for 1932 Fisher bodies were offered on the V-12 chassis, in addition to the original, semi-custom Fleetwood coachwork. This cut the cost of the least expensive sedan by $300, though the price of the Fleetwood job was increased by a couple of hundred dollars. But nothing helped. Despite Washington's assurance that prosperity was "just around the corner," 1932 proved to be the most dismal year the American economy has ever experienced. Sales of the Cadillac V-12 fell through the floor to 1,709 units, an astounding 70 percent drop. And the V-16's record was even more dismal with just 296 of these top-of-the-line Cadillacs finding buyers.

Nor did 1933 bring the country any

closer to that elusive "corner" around which prosperity was supposedly hiding. Certainly, that year did not treat Cadillac kindly, with sales of the V-12 sinking to 952 and those of the V-16 to a measly 125!

Major changes were undertaken for 1934. A boost in the compression ratio from 5.3:1 to 6.00:1 helped to increase the V-12's horsepower from 135 to 150. Hotchkiss drive replaced the earlier torque tube, contributing to a reduction in unsprung weight. There was a new dual X-type frame, and independent front suspension was adopted, contrubuting substantially to a more comfortable ride — and again, resulting in less unsprung weight (see sidebar, page 18).

This time, Fisher bodies were confined to the V-8 chassis. The V-12s, as well as the V-16s, were fitted only with the semi-custom Fleetwood coachwork. Cadillac evidently abandoned the idea of trying to make a profit by increasing

1935 CADILLAC

volume in its premium lines. The least expensive 1934 five-passenger sedan on the V-12 chassis sold for $3,995, compared to $3,595 for the Fisher-bodied 1933 model.

Styling was completely revamped, taking on a much more streamlined appearance than before. The slightly vee'd, fine-textured grille, shared by the V-8 and V-12 models, was smartly slanted. "Pontoon" fenders provided a massive look, and "bi-plane" bumpers added an art deco touch. These consisted of a pair of thin, chrome-plated blades, separated by a pair of "bullets," similar but for their more modest size to the "Dagmars" that became popular 20 years or so later. (These bumpers were one of the most attractive features of the 1934 Cadillacs and LaSalles. Unfortunately, they proved to be easily damaged and extremely difficult to repair and were dropped after only one season.)

Forward-opening front doors were featured by most body styles, and except for cars equipped with the extra-cost sidemounts, the spare tire was tucked neatly away in a locker at the rear. Only a few styles, such as the convertible sedan shown here, had built-in trunks with any significant carrying capacity. Most sedans were "flatbacks," with room in the rear compartment for the spare tire but very little else. It is noteworthy, however, that Cadillac and LaSalle shared with Hudson and Terraplane the distinction of being the first to carry the spare tire inside the car, a practice that soon became very nearly universal.

An astonishing proliferation of 52 body styles was catalogued for the V-12 chassis, with prices ranging from $3,995 for the base five-passenger sedan to $6,295 for the seven-passenger town cabriolet. Sixteen of these were shown with flat, one-piece windshields, while the others featured smart, two-piece vee'd glass. The latter cars were considered the premium models; where comparable types were available with either configuration, the split windscreen cars commanded a premium of about $500.

These must have been discouraging times for Larry Fisher, and for Nicholas Dreystadt, who succeeded Fisher as

specifications

illustrations by Russell von Sauers, The Graphic Automobile Studio

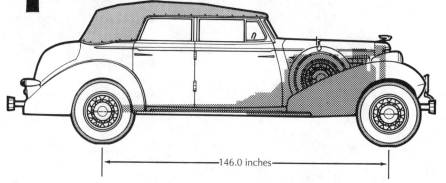

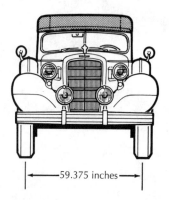

—146.0 inches—

—59.375 inches—

1935 Cadillac V-12 Convertible Sedan

Model	#5780 Convertible Sedan with divider window, 5-passenger
Original price	$4,995 f.o.b. factory
Options on dR car	White sidewall tires, fender wells with dual sidemounted spares and metal tire covers and mirrors, goddess radiator ornament, Trippe driving lights, radio, exhaust extensions, "banjo" steering wheel

ENGINE

Type	45-degree overhead-valve V-12
Bore and stroke	3.125 inches x 4 inches
Displacement	368.2 cubic inches
Compression ratio	6.00:1
Horsepower @ rpm	150 @ 3,600
Torque @ rpm	N/A
Taxable horsepower	46.9
Valve lifters	Mechanical; hydraulic valve silencers
Crankshaft	Counterbalanced; vibration damper
Main bearings	4
Fuel system	Two 1.5-inch single updraft Detroit Lubricator carburetors, mechanical pump
Lubrication system	Full pressure
Cooling system	Centrifugal pump
Exhaust system	Dual
Electrical system	6-volt battery/coil

CLUTCH

Type	Double plate
Diameter	10 inches
Actuation	Mechanical, foot pedal

TRANSMISSION

Type	3-speed selective, synchronized 2nd and 3rd gears, floor-mounted lever
Ratios: 1st	2.40:1
2nd	1.47:1
3rd	1.00:1
Reverse	2.49:1

DIFFERENTIAL

Type	Spiral bevel
Ratio	4.80:1
Drive axles	3/4 floating
Torque medium	Springs

STEERING

Type	Jacox worm-and-roller
Ratio	N/a
Turns lock-to-lock	3.875
Turning diameter	44 feet, six inches

BRAKES

Type	4-wheel internal mechanical
Drum diameter	15 inches
Effective area	237.7 square inches

CONSTRUCTION

Type	Body-on-frame
Frame	Dual X-type
Body construction	Composite, steel over wood framing
Body style	Convertible sedan
Coachbuilder	Fleetwood

SUSPENSION

Front	Independent, coil springs
Rear	Rigid axle, 66-inch x two 14-inch longitudinal leaf springs, torsional stabilizer
Wheels	Steel wire
Tires	7.50/17 6 ply

WEIGHTS AND MEASURES

Wheelbase	146 inches
Overall length	216 inches
Overall width	77 inches
Overall height	71 inches
Front track	59.375 inches
Rear track	62 inches
Min. road clearance	8.75 inches
Shipping weight	5,800 pounds

CAPACITIES

Crankcase	9 quarts
Cooling system	4.5 gallons
Fuel tank	30 gallons
Transmission	4.5 pounds
Differential	6 pounds

CALCULATED DATA

Hp per c.i.d.	.407
Weight (lb.) per hp	38.7
Weight per c.i.d.	15.8
P.S.I. (brakes)	24.4

Slightly vee'd windshield began on 1934 body designs as well.

1935 CADILLAC

Cadillac's general manager on June 1, 1934, for nothing they did was successful in stimulating sales. Production for 1934 dropped again, to only 683 V-12s and just 56 V-16s. Even the V-8s weren't doing well, with output totaling only 5,080 units – down from 40,000 during the record 1928 season.

As for 1935, despite a slight pickup in the nation's economy, Cadillac sales dropped even further, to 3,209 eights, 377 twelves and a scant 50 sixteens. That's just 3,636 Cadillacs produced for the 1935 model year, compared to

6,894 of the senior Packard Eights, Super-Eights and Twelves. (The reader will recall that by this time the LaSalle had ceased to be a Cadillac clone. Abandoning the luxury field in 1934, it had introduced a high-styled, Oldsmobile-based straight-eight, selling – by 1935 – for as little as $1,255, about a hundred dollars less than the Series 60 Buick.)

Clearly, Cadillac had reached a turning point. Something would have to change radically if the marque were to survive! How Nick Dreystadt and his staff managed to turn things around would (and did) require a book. Suffice it to say that by 1941 Cadillac was by far this nation's (and many would say

the world's) premier luxury automobile.

Driving Impressions

The fact that the 12-cylinder Cadillac failed to sell well in the depressed market of the 1930s is certainly no reflection on the quality of the automobile. The V-12 had its share of shortcomings, and we'll get to those presently, but basically it was an excellent machine, the product of sound engineering and superb, painstaking craftsmanship in both body and running gear. But like a lot of other fine cars, it was the victim of hard times.

The car that serves as our drive-Report subject is a particularly rare model, combining the flair of a four-door convertible with the formality of a divider window. Exactly how many cars of this type were produced we do not know, but given that only 377 V-12s were produced for 1935, most of them sedans of one sort or another, the total could not have been very great.

This model, along with the town sedans, served as a bellwether for its manufacturer, in the sense that these were the first Cadillacs to offer a genuine built-in trunk. By the following year, virtually every Cadillac sedan would be so equipped.

Dick De Luna, a San Mateo, California, businessman and avid collector of fine automobiles, purchased his Cadillac in January 1990 from an Arizona classic car dealer. Nothing is

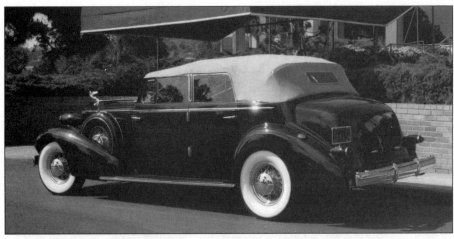

*Facing page: For a big, long, heavy car the Cad has less body lean in corners than we expected. **This page, above:** By 1935 all Cadillac bodies had grown prominent trunks except for a few closed models. **Below left:** Sidemount spares hide deep in skirted fenders. **Below right:** Not just one, but two handles open and close trunk.*

known of its early history, except that it was sold originally by Nolan Peeler Motors, Inc., of Miami, and there is evidence that at some point it was owned in southern California.

De Luna rebuilt the front end and overhauled the brakes. However, the factory-supplied vacuum booster is missing. We'll have something to say about that presently.

Dick was delighted to find that the V-12 engine was in basically good condition when he bought the car, although the valley pan and a few small parts such as knurled nuts were missing. Otherwise, the only problem in the engine compartment had to do with the exhaust manifolds. Someone had repaired them using the wrong kind of welding rod, which caused some stretch-

Luxury Twelves Compared

During 1935, four of America's automakers offered luxurious and expensive twelve-cylinder cars. In the interest of comparability, specifications of five-passenger sedans are shown here.

	Cadillac 370-D	Lincoln K-541	Packard Twelve	Pierce-Arrow 1245
Price, f.o.b. factory	$3,995	$4,600	$3,960	$3,295
Shipping weight	5,735 pounds	5,680 pounds	5,700 pounds	5,233 pounds
Wheelbase	146 inches	136 inches	139 inches	139 inches
Engine c.i.d.	368.2	414.2	473.4	461.8
Bore	3.125 inches	3.125 inches	3.44 inches	3.5 inches
Stroke	4 inches	4.5 inches	4.25 inches	4 inches
Stroke/bore ratio	1.28:1	1.44:1	1.24:1	1.14:1
Angle of cylinder banks	45-degree	67-degree	67-degree	80-degree
Horsepower/rpm	150/3,600	150/3,400	175/3,200	175/3,400
Compression ratio	6.00:1	6.38:1	6.40:1	6.00:1
Main bearings	4	4	4	7
Carburetion	2-updraft	Dual downdraft	Dual downdraft	2-downdraft
Clutch	Double plate	Single plate	Single plate	Double plate
Trans. ratios: 1-2	2.40-1.47	2.91-1.78	2.45-1.52	2.83-1.70
Differential	Spiral bevel	Spiral bevel	Hypoid	Hypoid
Final drive ratio	4.80:1	4.58:1	4.41:1	4.21:1
Steering	Worm/roller	Worm/roller	Worm/roller	Cam/lever
Brakes	Mechanical	Mechanical	Mechanical	Mechanical
Drum diameter	15 inches	15.125 inches	15 inches	16 inches
Braking area (sq. inches)	237.7	340.0	283.7	342.0
Tire size	7.50/17	7.50/17	7.50/17	7.50/17
Horsepower/c.i.d.	.407	.362	.370	.379
Weight/horsepower (lb.)	38.2	37.9	32.6	29.9
Weight/c.i.d.	15.6	13.7	12.0	11.3
Weight/sq. in. (brakes)	24.1	16.7	20.1	15.3

1935 CADILLAC

Imposing grille design evolved from first vee'd style front on 1933 Cadillacs. Even the 1934-'36 LaSalles with their distinctive tall, narrow grilles carry a family resemblance to this basic look. Tiny parking lamps are almost hidden under headlamps.

ing and thus a certain amount of leakage.

The body was in excellent condition except for a few missing parts, such as the divider window, door checks, ashtray and clock. Fortunately, Dick was able to locate replacements for all the missing pieces. It was necessary to have rubber weatherstrip channels specially made, but the top was in excellent condition. The wheels needed repainting; otherwise the finish, which is an authentic Cadillac color, needed only minor touch-up. A new set of white sidewall tires and a pair of Trippe driving lights completed the cosmetic restoration.

Although this car took a second-place award at the 1992 Hillsborough Concours d'Elegance, and was shown at Silverado 1992, it is not, strictly speak-

"Knee Action"

American automakers were faced with two seemingly unrelated challenges during the early 1930s. First, roads were rapidly being improved, and cars were much faster than before – and becoming more powerful with every passing year. Even Cadillac, traditionally among the most conservative firms in the business, advanced the output of its justly famed V-8 engine from 85.5 horsepower in 1927 to 115 five years later, a difference of 34.5 percent. This, of course, brought about a corresponding increase in the car's top speed. The open types would readily do better than 80 miles an hour by 1932, and even the sedans were good for an honest 75.

Unfortunately, unsprung weight was excessive, and the front-end structure lacked sufficient rigidity, even with the heavy frame reinforced by two box sections. Factory test crews – not to mention the proud owners of new Cadillacs – found that at the new, higher speeds there was a pronounced tendency for the front wheels to shimmy, particularly when any irregularity was detected in the pavement. Hard bumps tended to make the car skitter sideways, and any dip in the road produced an uncomfortable pitching sensation.

And that was challenge number one: Something needed to be done in order to improve the handling.

During this time women were taking the wheel of the family car in ever-increasing numbers. And what they wanted was a smoother, more comfortable ride, as well as easier steering. And that, to some of the more forward-looking automotive engineers, suggested independent front suspension.

Challenge number two!

In November 1930, a former Rolls-Royce engineer named Maurice Olley had joined the Cadillac staff. His assignment was direct enough, yet hardly a simple one: He was charged with smoothing out the ride

of the automobile.

Now, independent front suspension was not really a new idea at that time. Certain European manufacturers, notably Mercedes-Benz and Lancia, had employed it in one form or another, for several years, and there had been experiments on this side of the Atlantic as well. In 1931 Andre Dubonnet, heir to the French aperitif fortune, had patented a sealed hydraulic system, and at about the same time Cadillac engineers, under Maurice Olley's leadership, had turned their attention to the development of the now-familiar "wishbone" type.

Other designs were being devised as well. The Baker Axle Company was experimenting with an arrangement called the "articulated axle," which retained the conventional semi-elliptic springs but cut the axle in two, connecting the halves by means of a central parallelogram. By 1934 the Baker axle, sometimes called "Axleflex," would be featured as optional equipment by both Hudson and Nash. But not for long, for it proved to have a nasty habit of snapping spring leaves under hard use.

At Studebaker, meanwhile, chief engineer "Barney" Roos was working on his "Planar" design, preparing it for introduction on the 1935 models. In this instance a transverse leaf spring took the place of the coils usually associated with the wishbone suspension. Some owners, including this writer, complained of the difficulty of keeping the wheels in alignment, but Studebaker retained the system as late as 1949.

Times were tough in the thirties, of course, and competition was fierce. General Motors undertook to get one step ahead of its rivals by offering independent front suspension in all five of its 1934 car lines. Exhaustive tests of both the wishbone and Dubonnet systems had conclusively demonstrated the superiority of the former, especially when used with the heavier cars.

Unfortunately, the demand for these units outstripped the supply. Centerless grinding machines were needed to prepare the wire for the coil springs required by the wishbone suspension, and there weren't enough of these machines available to meet all of GM's requirements.

At that time (1934), Chevrolet was turning out two and a half times as many automobiles as the Buick, Oldsmobile, Pontiac and Cadillac Divisions combined. So the decision was made that Chevrolet would use the Dubonnet system, whose manufacture did not require the use of the centerless grinder, offering it as standard equipment on the Master series. And since Pontiac was sharing many of its components with Chevrolet, it too ended up with the Dubonnet suspension.

General Motors advertised both i.f.s. systems under the catchy title "Knee Action," and much was made of its virtues in the corporation's advertising program. The writer recalls seeing a 1934 Chevrolet in the showroom window, with one front wheel sitting on a four-inch block while the car's stance remained level. Down the street the Ford dealer, advertising "Free Action," jacked up the left front and right rear wheels of a display car in an effort to counter the Chevy demonstration. But it's doubtful that anyone was particularly impressed.

By 1937 Pontiac had replaced the Dubonnet setup with the much more serviceable wishbone suspension, and two years later Chevrolet followed suit. By 1941 it was standard equipment across the board, even in the least expensive Chevrolets.

Thus both dilemmas were solved. Unsprung weight was reduced and the shimmy and tramp that had been experienced with the I-beam front axle was gone. And riding comfort had been enhanced beyond anything the public had imagined just a few years earlier.

Left: Courtesy lamp for rear seat passengers. Below left: Balanced dash grouped all gauges directly before driver. Above: Rearward opening doors assist ease of entry to front area. Above right: This black box was an early attempt at improved radio reception.

ing, a "show" car. De Luna and his family regard it as a "driver," and have taken it on a number of excursions. Beyond that, it has been used in connection with several weddings.

Not unexpectedly, we found the big V-12 to be an exceptionally comfortable car. Seats are firm and supportive, and there's plenty of room, front and rear, for six-footers. The ride is soft without being mushy, and the Cad doesn't lean as much in the turns as we had anticipated.

But although the engine is smooth and quiet, it is not as powerful as we expected. We took the car for a fairly extended drive up and down the hills of San Mateo and nearby Burlingame. We have driven a Cadillac V-16 over similar terrain, and were greatly impressed by the effortless manner in which it sailed over even very steep grades. The twelve, on the other hand, wants to be downshifted. It's not short on horsepower, but the low-end torque is simply no match for some of the other big cars we've driven.

(The figures bear this out, by the way. Although the Cadillac V-12's 150 horsepower exactly matches that of the Lincoln V-12, its 265 foot-pounds of torque falls 15 percent short of the Lincoln's 312.)

Steering, while not excessively slow, is very heavy. The lady at our house

Fifty-Two To Choose From!

For 1935, Cadillac offered an astonishing array of 52 body styles on the V-12 chassis, 16 with flat windshields, 36 with the fashionable split windscreen, seen here on our driveReport car. Since just 52 V-12s were built during the model year, all of them bearing semi-custom bodies by Fleetwood, it is safe to say that relatively few – perhaps 20 – of the 52 styles were actually built. Here's the total roster, with prices available:

Flat windshield models:

6030-B	Imperial Sedan, 5-passenger	------
6030-FL	Imperial Cabriolet, 5-passenger	$4,395
6030-FM	Imperial Brougham, 5-passenger	------
6030-S	Sedan, 5-passenger	$3,995
6033-S	Town Sedan, 5-passenger	$4,045
6035	Convertible Coupe, 2-passenger	------
6075	Imperial Sedan, 7-passenger	$4,345
6075-B	Limousine (special back), 7-passenger	------
6075-D	Limousine, 7-passenger	------
6075-E	Limousine, 7-passenger	------
6075-FL	Imperial Cabriolet, 7-passenger	$4,545
6075-FM	Imperial Brougham, 7-passenger	------
6075-H3	Limousine, 7-passenger	------
6075-H4	Limousine, 7-passenger	------
6075-O	Imperial Sedan, 7-passenger	------
6075-S	Sedan, 7-passenger	$4,145

Vee windshield models:

5702	Roadster, 2-passenger	------
5712-C	Collapsible Town Cabriolet, 5-passenger	------
5712-LB	Town Cabriolet, 5-passenger	$6,195
5712-MB	Town Cabriolet, 5-passenger	------
5720	Town Cabriolet, 7-passenger	------
5720-C	Collapsible Town Cabriolet, 7-passenger	------
5725-B	Town Cabriolet, 7-passenger	------
5725-LB	Town Cabriolet, 7-passenger	$6,295
5725-MB	Town Cabriolet, 7-passenger	------
5730	Imperial Sedan, 5-passenger	------
5730-FL	Imperial Sedan, 5-passenger	$4,845
5730-FM	Imperial Brougham, 5-passenger	------
5730-S	Sedan, 5-passenger	$4,445
5733	Imperial Town Sedan, 5-passenger	------
5733-S	Town Sedan, 5-passenger	$4,995
5735	Convertible Coupe, 2-passenger	$4,745
5757	Touring, 7-passenger	------
5759	Sport Phaeton, 5-passenger	------
5775	Imperial Sedan (Limousine), 7-passenger	$4,795
5775-B	Limousine, 7-passenger	------
5775-E	Imperial Sedan, 7-passenger	------
5775-FL	Imperial Cabriolet, 7-passenger	$4,995
5775-FM	Imperial Brougham, 7-passenger	------
5775-H4	Imperial Sedan, 7-passenger	------
5775-S	Sedan, 7-passenger	$4,595
5775-W	Limousine, 7-passenger	------
5776	Coupe, 2-passenger	$4,595
5780	Convertible Sedan/divider window, 5-passenger	$4,995
5780-B	Convertible Sedan, 5-passenger	------
5780-S	Convertible Sedan, 5-passenger	------
5785	Collapsible Coupe, 5-passenger	$4,995
5788	Stationary Coupe, 5-passenger	------
5789-A	Victoria Coupe, 4-passenger	------
5791	Limousine Brougham, 7-passenger	$6,195
5791-B	Limousine Brougham, 7-passenger	------
5799	Aerodynamic Coupe, 5-passenger	$4,995

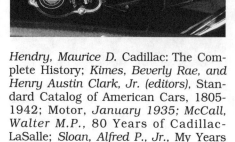

Left: *The mighty ohv V-12 develops 150 bhp.* Below left: *Instruments include a display for the three-beam headlamps.* Below: *Cadillac's carb supplier also built units for Packard.* Bottom left: *Center-hinged doors have potential for colliding with each other.* Right: *Open areas on each side of hood are needed to clear vents.* Bottom: *Cadillac styling was among the most advanced of the luxury cars in 1935.*

1935 CADILLAC

would find parking this car an almost impossible task, although at speed it is not particularly difficult to handle. The clutch chatters just slightly and if gears are shifted too rapidly the synchronizers can be over-ridden, but these presumably are signs of normal wear, rather than of any design flaw.

In at least one respect, Cadillac was behind the times in 1935. By that time hydraulic brakes had been adopted by the LaSalle, the division's lower-priced "companion" car. The Cadillac retained its traditional mechanical binders for this one final year, and we found that, minus that all-important vacuum booster, they require a great deal of pedal pressure in order to bring the car to a halt. Even with a booster they have their work cut out for them, handling 24.4 pounds of automobile for every square inch of effective area. Contributing to the problem is the fact that these brakes are identical in lining area to those of the Fisher-bodied Cadillac V-8s, cars which in some cases weigh as much as three-quarters of a ton less than our driveReport car.

There would be better days ahead for Cadillac when the 1936 models were introduced. By that time the economy had picked up somewhat, and paced by the new Series 60, the division's overall sales would come to two and a half times their 1935 total. In the V-12 line, the new model would be eight inches shorter and 700 pounds lighter than its 1935 counterpart – and of course, correspondingly more nimble. Happily, it would also be about $650 cheaper, thanks in part to Dreystadt's notably frugal management. Sales of the 12-cylinder cars would increase by 139 percent during the 1936 season.

Altogether, 10,821 Cadillac V-12s were built between the start of production in mid-1930 and its termination,

seven years later. It's an impressive number, given the economic conditions of the time – nearly double rival Packard's total of 5,744 12-cylinder cars, manufactured over a similar time span, between 1931 and 1938. ❏

Acknowledgements and Bibliography

Automobile Trade Journal, March 1935; Automotive Industries, February 23, 1935; Carson, Richard Burns, The Olympian Cars; *Heasley, Jerry,* The Production Figure Book for US Cars; *Hendry, Maurice D.* Cadillac: The Complete History; *Kimes, Beverly Rae, and Henry Austin Clark, Jr. (editors),* Standard Catalog of American Cars, 1805-1942; *Motor, January 1935; McCall, Walter M.P.,* 80 Years of Cadillac-LaSalle; *Sloan, Alfred P., Jr.,* My Years with General Motors.

Our thanks to Dave Brown, Durham, California; Maury O'Hearn, San Mateo, California; Walter M.P. McCall, Windsor, Ontario, Canada. Special thanks to Dick De Luna, San Mateo, California.

Last Battle for a Diminishing Market

1939 Cadillac V-16 vs. 1939 Packard Twelve

Originally published in Special Interest Autos #138, Nov.-Dec. 1993

by Arch Brown
photos by Roy Query

THROUGHOUT the decade of the thirties, while Chevrolet and Ford were engaged in a pitched battle for supremacy in the low-priced field, an equally intense contest was taking place at the opposite end of the economic scale. Cadillac was determined to dislodge Packard from its long-held status as America's premier luxury automobile. And Packard was equally determined to retain its position as "King of the Mountain."

Matters might be said to have come to a head on January 4, 1930, at the New York Automobile Show, when Cadillac upstaged the rest of the industry by showing off a magnificent new sixteen-cylinder motorcar. It was a formidable challenge to the competition, for nothing comparable had ever before been offered to the public.

Nineteen-thirty was not a propitious time for Cadillac — or anyone else, for that matter — to introduce a line of automobiles whose prices ranged from $5,350 to $9,700, enough in those days to pay for a small fleet of ordinary motorcars. For the bottom had fallen out of the stock market the previous October, and hard times were commencing to make themselves felt. But of course, at that point nobody could have anticipated how deep and how long the Depression would be, and in any case, by the time of the Wall Street debacle it was much too late to cancel the V-16.

The challenge to the rest of the industry, and especially to Packard, was unmistakable. One can be certain that out on Detroit's East Grand Boulevard, the men at Packard paid close attention to the reception accorded this great new Cadillac. Long regarded as America's leading prestige car, for several years Packard had been under increasing pressure from Cadillac, its principal competitor. The 1929 introduction of the LaSalle, priced nose-to-nose with the least expensive Packards, had intensified the competition in that segment of the market. And now, here was Cadillac with a sixteen-cylinder "super-car."

Packard, of course, was not unfamiliar with the multi-cylinder game. Between 1915 and 1923 the company had built a superb 90-horsepower V-12 called the Twin Six. Selling for half-again as much as the contemporary Cadillac, this was the car that had established Packard's supremacy in the high-priced market. Yet it was the Single Six, a smaller, more reasonably priced machine introduced in 1920,

Both Cadillac and Packard made sure the number of cylinders under the hood was announced on their wheel covers.

that had accounted for the bulk of Packard's volume for the next several years.

By 1924 the Twin Six had been replaced by the Single Eight, a straight-eight that was just as big and nearly as powerful as the twelve-cylinder car, but not quite as expensive. Together with the Single Six, it pushed Packard's 1925 production to 32,125 cars, com-

pared to Cadillac's total of 22,542.

With Cadillac's introduction of its "companion" car, the LaSalle, in mid-1927, the sales gap narrowed somewhat. By 1928 production figures came to 50,054 for Packard, 41,172 for Cadillac and LaSalle combined. Which was all well and good, but it was primarily upon the high-priced models that each company's prestige depended; and ap-

23

Cadillac's mascot has an aggressive look to it, while Packard's traditional pelican is all curves and grace. **Facing page:** Both cars have an appearance of dignity and bank-vault solidity.

SIA comparisonReport

parently, in the public's mind more status was attached to the 109 horsepower Packard straight-eight than to the 90 horsepower Cadillac.

To Lawrence P. Fisher, Cadillac's general manager since 1925, such a situation was intolerable; and with his encouragement work got under way in 1926 on the development of the V-16. The operation was carried out in the deepest secrecy. Blueprints, supplies and equipment were all labeled "Bus," or "Coach," and rumors were deliber-

ately floated that a new V-12 would be forthcoming. (In fact, there *was* a V-12, developed simultaneously with the V-16 but introduced some months later. But the big secret had to do with the sixteen-cylinder job.)

In overall charge of the V-16 project was the division's chief engineer, Ernest Seaholm; while development of the great new engine was the responsibility of Owen Nacker, a former Marmon engineer. Unlike the familiar Cadillac V-8, which was of L-head design, the V-16 used overhead valves. Quiet operation was assured by means of hydraulic valve silencers, and smoothness was enhanced by the even firing order, resulting from placement of the cylinder

banks at a 45-degree angle to one another.

No question about it: In terms of both power and prestige, the Cadillac V-16 was well ahead of anything Packard had to offer at the time. Performance was outstanding. Displacing 452 cubic inches, the new engine was rated at 165 horsepower; and it was said to be capable of propelling the heavy Cadillacs to speeds ranging from 80 to nearly 100 miles an hour, depending on body contours, gear ratio and the weight of the coachwork.

The V-16 was also one of the handsomest powerplants ever devised. Walter McCall has described it as "the first automobile engine anywhere to bear the mark of a stylist." Wires and hoses were hidden away; valve covers were trimmed in ribbed, polished aluminum; surfaces were finished in black enamel, with bright accents.

Obviously, a response from Packard was called for. It took the form of a new Twin Six, augmenting the company's Eight and Eight Deluxe lines, and introduced as a member of the Ninth Series on June 17, 1931. (Packard, in those days, identified its cars not by model year, like the rest of the industry, but by series number.) With its vee'd radiator grille, tapered headlamps and aircraft-style instrument panel, this highstyled car established the pattern for the Tenth Series Packards, slated for display early in January 1933.

Presumably, consideration must have been given to matching Cadillac, cylinder-for-cylinder. But the old Twin Six had enjoyed a well-established reputation for both performance and durability, and whatever advantages a sixteen-cylinder engine may have enjoyed over a twelve were no more than marginal — and might be thought to have been offset by the increased complexity of the V-16 layout, to say nothing of the additional cost of producing it. So the decision was made that Packard's response to Cadillac would be another twelve-cylinder car.

Such was the status accorded Packard in those days that when the second-generation Twin Six was introduced, the news flashed across the ticker tape on Wall Street. Even so, there were few in those troubled times who could afford a new automobile of any kind, least of all a costly luxury model. Despite offering four lines of cars for 1932 — three eights in addition to the Twin Six — Packard's production came to just 8,018 units, an 84 percent drop from 1928's record total. Packard, along with Cadillac, found itself building superb automobiles for a market that had virtually ceased to exist. In order to survive, both firms began to think in terms of developing lower-priced cars. Not that either Packard or Cadillac was prepared to abandon the

1930-1940 Production
Packard Twin Six/Twelve and Cadillac V-16/V-12
(Model year figures shown)

		Packard Twin Six/Twelve	Cadillac V-16	Cadillac V-12
1930-31		-----	3,250	5,725
1932	(9th Series)	549	296	1,709
1933	(10th Series)	520	125	952
1934	(11th Series)	960	56	683
1935	(12th Series)	721	50	377
1936	(14th Series)	682	52	901
1937	(15th Series)	1,300	49	474
1938	(16th Series)	566	311	-----
1939	(17th Series)	446	136	-----
1940		-----	61	-----
Totals:		5,744	4,386	10,821

Note: Perhaps a fairer comparison would be to show only 1932-39, years in which Packard competed in the rarified multi-cylinder market. In that event the count looks like this:

Packard	5,744
Cadillac V-16	1,075
Cadillac V-12	5,096

Source: Heasley, Jerry, *The Production Figure Book for US Cars*

upper end of the market.

Packard's new twelve-cylinder engine, at 445.5 cubic inches and 160 horsepower, was very nearly a match for the Cadillac V-16 in terms of both displacement and horsepower. And it was a fresh development, rather than a derivative of the earlier Twin Six. This time the cylinder blocks were inclined at a 67-degree angle to one-another, rather than the 60-degree placement used for Packard's earlier 12-cylinder engine. That seems odd, when you think of it, since a 60- (or 120-) degree layout is required to provide a V-12 with precisely equal firing intervals. Any disadvantage resulting from this configuration is purely theoretical, however, for the second Twin-Six engine ranks with the Cadillac V-16 as one of the smoothest engines ever designed.

At first, Packard employed custom and semi-custom coachwork exclusively, with prices starting at $5,800 for the Dietrich-bodied phaeton. This was about $700 lower than the Fleetwood-bodied V-16 in the same body style, though of course it was still beyond the reach of all but the very rich. Then in January 1932 the Twin Six line was expanded to include several factory-bodied styles, priced as low as $3,650 for the 2/4 passenger coupe. (This is not to suggest that $3,650 could be considered a "low" price, but by way of comparison, the Fleetwood-bodied Cadillac V-16 coupe sold, at that time, for $5,800.)

Not only was the Twin Six substantially less costly than the V-16, it was also several hundred pounds lighter. Thus, Packard enjoyed a distinct edge in terms of power-to-weight radio, as well as price. And while neither car could be called a hot ticket on the sales floor in those depressed times, the big Packard outsold the Cadillac V-16 by margins as high as four to one. (It should be noted, however, that the Cad V-12, introduced during October 1930, undoubtedly stole some sales that would otherwise have gone to the V-16.)

With the coming of the Tenth Series, on January 5, 1933, the Twin Six name was dropped, and the car was known thereafter as the Packard Twelve. The company was taking no chances that the public might look upon the twelve-cylinder engine as a warmed-over version of the 1915-23 unit, which was by then seriously outmoded. Sales were somewhat better than those of the Ninth Series, but at 520 units the volume fell far short of profitability. Production of the Cadillac V-16, meanwhile, hit a new low of 126 for the 1933 model year. Even the Cadillac V-12, somewhat less expensive than the Packard Twelve, found only 953 buyers that year.

Commencing with the introduction of the Twelfth Series, on August 30, 1934,

Packard's twelve-cylinder engine was stroked a quarter of an inch, raising its displacement to 473.4 cubic inches, and boosting the horsepower to 175. And then on January 5, 1935, Packard invaded the medium-priced field with the One-Twenty. (This was the company's second attempt at building a more moderately priced car, by the way. The first, known as the Ninth Series Light Eight, was dropped after only one year when it was found that it could only be sold at a loss; and worse, it stole sales from the potentially profitable Standard Eight, whose engine it shared.)

Not only did the One-Twenty (see *SIA* #47) sell for less than half the price of the cheapest senior model, known by that time simply as the Packard Eight; it incorporated some important engineering improvements that wouldn't be seen on the more expensive lines until the coming of 1937's Fifteenth Series. Perhaps the most important of these developments — certainly the most widely recognized — were independent front suspension, featured by Cadillac since 1934; and hydraulic brakes, which Cadillac adopted a full year before the big Packards got around to it.

Nine months after the debut of the One-Twenty, Cadillac responded with its new Series Sixty (see *SIA* #69). Substantially higher in price than the One-Twenty, it managed nevertheless to undercut the cost of the cheapest 1935 Cadillac by nearly $800.

The One-Twenty and the Series Sixty promptly became the volume lines for their respective manufacturers, while the classic models were produced in minuscule numbers. Cadillac, especially, faced bitterly disappointing sales of its twelve- and sixteen-cylinder cars, though the LaSalle and the Cadillac "60" were doing well. During 1937, a relatively good year for the industry,

General Motors was able to sell only 50 Cadillac V-16s and 478 V-12s, compared to 13,636 Cadillac V-8s and 32,005 LaSalles. Packard did somewhat better in the luxury department, with 1,300 Twelves leaving the factory. But it was the medium-priced Packards, the One-Twenty and the newly introduced six-cylinder One-Fifteen, that accounted for 94 percent of the company's volume and probably all of its profit for the year.

With the arrival of the Fifteenth Series, in September 1936, Packard's senior lines were reduced by one. On paper, it was the Eight that had been eliminated, while both the Super Eight and the Twelve were retained in the line. Closer examination reveals, however, that the Fifteenth Series Super Eight borrowed the engine of the Fourteenth Series Eight, rather than that of the Super Eight — and its wheelbase as well. A bit of badge-engineering here, it appears.

Styling was little changed, except that the radiator shell was given a 30-degree slant and "suicide" front doors were no longer used on the factory bodies. The adoption of hydraulic brakes and independent front suspension provided greater safety and an even more comfortable ride. And thanks to the new front suspension, the heavy vibration dampening bumpers — previously a feature of the senior Packards — were no longer needed. They were replaced by a lighter, simpler design.

By this time, major product planning decisions had been made at both Cadillac and Packard. At Packard it had been determined that the Seventeenth Series Super Eight would be a smaller, lighter and much less expensive car than its predecessors — priced, in fact, to compete with the Cadillac Series Sixty. Plans also called for phasing out

Specifications: '39 Cadillac V-16 vs. '39 Packard Twelve

	1939 Cadillac V-16	1939 Packard Twelve
Base price	$6,000 f.o.b. factory w/ standard equipment	N/A (convertible sedan, $5,395)
Engine	135-degree, L-head V-16, cast en bloc	67-degree V-12, modified L-head, cast en bloc
Bore x stroke	3.25 x 3.25 inches	3.4375 x 4.25 inches
Displacement	431.4 cubic inches	473.4 cubic inches
Compression ratio	6.75:1	6.30:1
Horsepower @ rpm	185 @ 3,600	175 @ 3,200
Torque @ rpm	324 @ 1,700	N/A
Taxable horsepower	67.6	56.7
Main bearings	9	4
Fuel system	2 Carter dual downdraft carburetors, 2 camshaft pumps	Stromberg EE-3, 1.5-inch dual downdraft carburetor, mechanical pump
Lubrication system	Pressure	Pressure
Cooling system	2 centrifugal pumps	Centrifugal pump
Electrical system	6-volt battery/coil	6-volt battery/coil
Exhaust system	Single	Single
Clutch	Single dry plate	Single dry plate
Outside diameter	11.5 inches	12 inches
Actuation	Mechanical, foot pedal	Foot pedal, vacuum-assisted
Transmission	3-speed selective, synchro-nized 2nd and 3rd gears; column-mounted lever	3-speed selective, synchronized 2nd and 3rd gears; column-mounted lever
Ratios: 1st/2nd/3rd/Reverse	2.39/1.53/1.00/2.39	2.46/1.53/1.00/2.98
Differential	Hypoid	Hypoid
Ratio	4.31:1	4.41:1
Drive axles	Semi-floating	Semi-floating
Torque medium	Rear springs	Rear springs
Steering	Saginaw worm and double roller	Worm and roller, using needle bearings
Turning diameter	47 feet	45 feet
Turns, lock-to-lock	4.63	5
Brakes	4-wheel internal, drum type	4-wheel internal hydraulic drum type, vacuum-assisted
Drum diameter	14 inches	14 inches
Effective area	258 square inches	330 square inches
Chassis and body	Body-on-frame	Body-on-frame
Frame	Rigid X-type with reinforced side-members	Perimeter type with X-member
Body construction	All steel	Steel over wood framing
Body type	Convertible sedan	7-passenger phaeton
Front suspension	Independent, coil springs, torsion rod sway eliminator	Independent, coil springs, torque arms
Rear suspension	Rigid axle, 62-inch x 2.5-inch semi-elliptic springs cross-link sway eliminator	Rigid axle, 60.5-inch x 2.25-inch semi-elliptic springs
Shock absorbers	Double-acting hydraulic	Delco double-acting
Wheels	Pressed steel, drop--center rims	Steel disc, drop-center rims
Tires	7.50/16 6-ply	8.25/16 6-ply
Wheelbase	141 inches	139.375 inches
Overall length	220.625 inches	225.781 inches
Overall width	77.625 inches	74.75 inches
Overall height	69.625 inches	(convertible sedan), 67.44 inches
Front track	59 inches	59 inches
Rear track	62.5 inches	61 inches
Minimum road clearance	8 inches	9 inches
Shipping weight	5,350 pounds	(convertible sedan), 5,890 pounds
Crankcase capacity	11 quarts	10 quarts
Cooling system capacity	30 quarts	40 quarts
Fuel tank	26.5 gallons	30 gallons
Transmission	2.5 pounds	4.5 pints
Differential	6.5 pounds	6 pints
Horsepower/c.i.d.	.429	.370 (based on weight of conv sedan)
Lb./horsepower	28.9	33.7
Lb./c.i.d.	12.4	12.4
Lb./sq. in. brake area	20.7	17.8
Top speed	100 mph	N/A
Acceleration (high gear) 10-25	4.8 seconds	N/A
10-60 mph	16.0 seconds	N/A
Model year production	138 (Cadillac V-16)	446 (Packard Twelve)

26

the Twelve at the end of the 1939 season. There simply wasn't enough volume to justify the expense of tooling up for a new model; and Packard was preparing, however reluctantly, to withdraw from the super-luxury market.

Naturally, no public announcement was made of the forthcoming demise of the Packard Twelve. But to those who knew what to watch for, the signs were apparent enough. The huge, 144-inch-wheelbase models had disappeared at the end of the Fifteenth Series. Just fourteen body styles each were catalogued for the Sixteenth and Seventeenth Series, down from 24 in the Eleventh Series. And although ten of the 14 remaining models bore Packard factory bodies, all of them were produced on individual order only. The last of the great Packard Twelves left the factory on August 8, 1939. Cadillac had won the contest by default.

In a sense, however, it was a hollow victory. For although Cadillac underscored its status by introducing a completely redesigned Sixteen for 1938, the new model was destined to have a short life. Priced midway between the previous V-12 and V-16 Cadillacs, and intended to replace them both, this second-generation Supercar shared with the eight-cylinder Series 75 its freshly restyled Fleetwood bodies — 12 of them, ranging from a smart convertible coupe to a formal town car. In fact, apart from differences in the grille, hood louvers and some minor trim items, the V-16 could hardly be distinguished, visually, from the V-8. Except, that is, for its price tag, for it cost some $2,140 more than the eight-cylinder version. Put another way, for the price of a V-16 sedan the buyer could have a Series 75 Cadillac in the same body style, with a Buick Century convertible and a Master Deluxe Chevrolet thrown in for good measure. Since the eight-cylinder Cadillac was a thoroughly competent performer in its own right, it is small wonder that the V-16 ran into a wall of buyer resistance.

First year sales of the new model totaled just 315, which must have been a bitter disappointment to general manager Nick Dreystadt, and after that it was downhill all the way. Just 138 of these fine automobiles found buyers in 1939 and 61 in 1940. And when that season drew to a close, Cadillac gave up the struggle.

Still, the second-generation V-16 was an interesting car, and a fine piece of engineering. The original sixteen-cylinder engine had been very expensive to produce. Cylinder banks were cast separately, and of course a great deal of

time and attention had gone into the engine's appearance. It was a very tall engine, thanks to the combination of overhead valves and the narrow, 45-degree "Vee." Thus it was found to be quite unsuitable for the lower hood lines that were coming into fashion. Nor did it accommodate itself readily to downdraft carburetion.

The second-generation Cadillac V-16, in contrast, was a "square" engine, with bore and stroke each measuring 3¼ inches. The block was a single casting, with cylinder banks set at an angle of 135-degrees to one another, in what looked almost like a "pancake" layout. The new mill, six inches shorter, 13 inches lower and 250 pounds lighter than its predecessor, had fewer than half as many parts as the original V-16. Accordingly, it was a good deal cheaper to manufacture. The L-head configuration was used this time in lieu of overhead valves; and hydraulic valve lifters replaced the previous combination of mechanical lifters and hydraulic silencers. Displacement, at 431 cubic inches, was 4.6 percent smaller than the earlier type; yet horsepower remained at 185, same as the final edition of the ohv V-16. And if the L-head lacked the earlier V-16's remarkable good looks, it didn't matter very much; for thanks to its nearly flat shape together with its placement, low in the engine compartment, it wasn't particularly visible, anyway.

But the day of the "supercar" had passed. The Packard Twelve and the Cadillac V-16 were both relics of a bygone time, the like of which we shall never see again.

Driving Impressions

For our comparisonReport subjects, *SIA* called once again upon General William Lyon, who has in his Southern California collection a superb Packard Twelve phaeton and an equally fine Cadillac V-16 convertible sedan, both of 1939 vintage.

For many years Packard had been noted for its smartly styled phaetons; but by the mid-thirties demand for that body style had all but disappeared. Packard's last factory-bodied phaeton was a member of the Fourteenth Series, which may cause knowledgeable readers to wonder about the Seventeenth

*Above left: Packard rear-seat passengers enjoyed lots of leg room even with auxiliary seats up. **Above and below:** Caddy and Packard were no strangers to gas pumps. Caddy tank holds 26 gallons; Packard, 30.*

Series example pictured here. That's where the Derham Body Company, of Rosemont, Pennsylvania, comes in.

Founded in 1887 as a carriage-building enterprise, Derham became an early supplier of coachwork for fine motorcars. Prominent among its customers were the Packard distributors in Philadelphia and New York. And while Derham became known especially for its formal, chauffeur-driven body types, it also produced the occasional sport coupe — and during the thirties — some attractive open types.

As the Depression deepened and demand for custom-bodied automobiles dried up, one by one the famous coachbuilders closed their doors. Derham survived in large part by modifying factory bodies. In some instances sedans were converted to town cars; at other times softly padded tops were added, smaller rear windows were fitted, or the configuration of the greenhouse was altered.

In the case of our comparisonReport Packard, Derham worked its magic on a

convertible sedan, transforming it into the smart phaeton pictured here. How much the firm charged the original owner for this modification, we have no way of knowing. Today, the operation would be prohibitively expensive; but skilled labor was still comparatively cheap in 1939, so the cost may have been relatively reasonable. Added during the transformation was a pair of jump seats, not normally available in the convertible sedan. (Notice, by the way, how smoothly and neatly the top folds. Derham's workmanship, whatever it cost, was obviously of the highest quality.)

Our Fleetwood-bodied Cadillac, on the other hand, is strictly a stock example, though it is a very rare car. During the 1940 season, only four convertible sedans were built on the V-16 chassis, this one bearing body number four. The body is all-steel, in contrast to the Packard as well as the first-generation Cadillac V-16, both of which employed composite wood and steel construction.

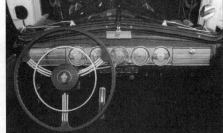

Above left: *Caddy's engine was nearly horizontally opposed at 135 degrees.* **Center:** *Packard's venerable Twelve debuted in 1932. This car is one of 446 built in '39, the engine's final year.* **Right:** *Derham was one of few coachbuilders to last past WW2.* **Below:** *Cadillac dash design is severely modern, while Packard retains more traditional appearance. Both cars display superb woodgraining.*

SIA comparisonReport

Partly as a result, the Cadillac is the lighter of these two cars by at least 500 pounds. (We can't give an exact figure, since we do not know the Packard's precise weight. It is safe to assume, however, that it doesn't vary much from that of the convertible sedan from which the phaeton was derived.)

The Packard had been treated during the mid-1980's to a thorough, four-year restoration by Richard Martin; while the Cadillac, purchased at auction during 1988, needed considerable mechanical work when General Lyon acquired it. A previous owner had gone through the engine and clutch, but hadn't made much of a job of it. Cylinder walls needed honing, and a ten-inch clutch plate had been installed instead of the 11.5-inch type specified by the factory. John Sobers, who maintains General Lyon's cars, replaced the rings and bearings and did a proper valve job, as well as installing the correct clutch. Today, both cars perform like new.

There is ample front leg room in both of these cars; and even the tallest rear-seat passengers are able to stretch their legs at full length. Seating, in both instances, is marvelously comfortable. The same is true of the ride; in both cases, the suspension is on the soft side, without being mushy.

We have found no performance statistics on these two cars; but beyond question the Cadillac, with a 16 percent advantage in power-to-weight ratio, is the quicker of the two. This is not to suggest that the Packard is any slouch. It's a fast, powerful automobile by any-

one's standards. Starting in top gear at ten miles an hour, we drive each of the cars up the long, winding, relatively steep driveway leading to the Lyon home. Both the Cadillac and the Packard picked up speed so rapidly that halfway to the top we had to ease off on the throttle.

In some respects, the Packard is the easier car to drive. Both clutch and brakes are power-assisted, so only minimal pedal pressure is required. The Packard also has substantially greater braking area than the Cadillac, which uses the same binders as the lighter, less powerful Series 75 V-8. So the advantage goes to Packard in this respect.

Neither car is built for hard cornering. These are luxury cars, after all, not hot rods; and they lean over rather sharply in fast turns. Steering effort, though considerable, is somewhat less than we expected, given the weight of these machines. The Packard has the advantage of needle bearings in the steering mechanism. But the Cadillac, in addition to being a quarter of a ton lighter, uses smaller-diameter tires. The result, it seems to us, is about a stand-off in terms of steering ease. (Robert E. Turnquist, writing in *The Packard Story,* observes that "Although the Twelve was fitted with 8.25 x 16 super cushions, the 7.50 x 16 six-ply gives it better handling qualities and the interchange is recommended.")

Both cars are fitted with steering-column gearshift controls, standard equipment on the Cadillac since 1938 and available as a $240 option on the Seventeenth Series Packards. In both instances shifts are easy, though the

Packard's linkage is tighter and its action somewhat more precise. Both transmissions are synchronized on second and top gears. A few of the Packard Twelves in this series were built with vacuum-assisted gearshift mechanisms, but this car is not one of them.

Both engines are counterbalanced for smoothness, and both are whisper-quiet but, thanks to its use of composite construction, sound insulation is better in the Packard. The result is that, without taking anything away from the Cadillac, the Packard has a slightly more luxurious "feel" than its rival.

So, which to choose, if this were 1939 and we were given that option?

Hard to say, for the answer really depends upon one's priorities. The Cadillac is a much later design than the Packard. There's an immediate awareness of the difference in both styling and performance. The Cad is faster, livelier, a little nimbler than its competitor. On the other hand, there's a hard-to-describe "feel" of luxury in the Packard that the Cadillac can't quite match and, despite styling that was already four years old when this car was built, it was still, in 1939 — and remains today — an exceptionally handsome automobile. Packard also has the advantage in cost: Comparing stock convertible sedans, in 1939 the Packard was priced about $600 below the Cadillac. Were the Cadillac's four additional cylinders worth the price of a new Chevrolet business coupe?

Perhaps not, as far as we are concerned, but that's a personal judgment, and a highly subjective one. 🪶

Acknowledgments and Bibliography

Automobile Trade Journal, *August 1939;* Automotive Industries, *February 25, 1939;* Cadillac Motor Car Division factory literature; Carson, Richard Burns, The Olympian Cars; Hendry, Maurice D., Cadillac: The Complete History; Kimes, Beverly Rae (ed.), Packard: A History of the Motorcar and the Company; McCall, Walter M.P., Eighty Years of Cadillac/LaSalle; Packard Motor Car Company factory literature; Pfau, Hugo, The Coachbuilt Packard; Schneider, Roy A., Sixteen-Cylinder Motorcars; Taylor, Frank, "Packard's Legendary Giants: The V-12 Series of 1932-39." Packard Illustrated, Spring 1975; Turnquist, Robert E., The Packard Story; "Packard," Fortune, January 1937.

Our thanks to Vic Fink, Hillsborough, California; Allan Jones, Byron, Califor-

Accessory trunk gives Packard a bit more flash at the back compared to Caddy.

Above and Below: Both cars develop bagsful of torque at low rpm for impressive high-gear performance.

nia; Bud Juneau, Brentwood, California; Janet Ross, Librarian, National Automobile Museum, Reno, Nevada; John Sobers, Trabuco Canyon, California. Special thanks to General William Lyon, Newport Beach, California.

1939

It was, in many ways, a pivotal year.

In some respects, it was a time for celebration. During June, Britain's King George VI and Queen Elizabeth, parents of the present monarch, paid a visit to the United States and Canada. Great International Expositions were held that year at either end of the continent, one opening in San Francisco on February 18, the other staged in New York, commencing on April 30. Exhibits ranged from Sally Rand's tantalizing fan dancers and Billy Rose's spectacular Aquacade, to sophisticated science demonstrations that gave the world an intriguing glimpse into the future. It was, at least superficially, a happy time.

But still, the signs were ominous. Americans were altogether too well aware that Hitler's troops had marched into Austria during March of the previous year. Six months later, having virtually handed Czechoslovakia over to the Nazis, Britain's Prime Minister, Neville Chamberlain, had naively proclaimed "Peace in Our Time." But Germany was not among the 60 or so nations that participated in our two World's Fairs, and in our hearts we knew that for the long run there could be no peace. With dread we anticipated the sound of the opening salvos. We hadn't long to wait, for Hitler's invasion of Poland followed on September 1, 1939, and Europe was at war once more.

Meanwhile, despite whatever anxieties we may have felt, most of us here in the United States experienced little change in our lifestyles. We were reminded by the isolationists among us that two great oceans protected our shores, and the possibility of attack — not to speak of invasion — seemed very remote. So we read John Steinbeck's *The Grapes of Wrath* and contemplated the plight of the Dust Bowl refugees. We marveled when Captain James W. Chapman,

Jr., of the Army Air Corps, piloted his plane from Washington, DC, to Moscow and return in just five days, one hour and 55 minutes' flying time. And we were outraged when the Daughters of the American Revolution, citing her race as their reason, barred Marian Anderson — arguably America's greatest contralto — from giving a concert in Constitution Hall. (An open-air concert in Lincoln Memorial Park was quickly arranged by a committee which included First Lady Eleanor Roosevelt, and a crowd of 75,000 people turned out to hear Miss Anderson sing.)

On Broadway we watched as *Life With Father* opened what would become a record-breaking eight-year run, totaling 3,224 performances. And in the realm of popular music we listened to Tommy Dorsey's hit recording of "I'll Never Smile Again," The Ink Spots' interpretation of "If I Didn't Care," and Benny Goodman's rendition of "I Didn't Know What Time It Was." We heard Kate Smith sing Irving Berlin's "God Bless America," little knowing that in time it would become virtually a second National Anthem.

Baseball turned 100 that year, according to the reckoning of Cooperstown, New York, where the game is said to have originated. The New York Yankees, paced by Joe DiMaggio, celebrated the occasion by beating Cincinnati 4-0 in the World Series; and DiMaggio, to nobody's surprise, was designated the American League's Most Valuable Player.

The movies, too, provided a welcome escape, featuring pictures like *The Wizard of Oz*, with 16-year-old Judy Garland heading a superb all-star cast. Then there was a delightful political satire called *Mr. Smith Goes to Washington*, starring Jimmy Stewart and Jean Arthur. *The Women*, consisting of Norma Shearer, Joan Crawford, and Rosalind Russell, may have foretold the

coming of feminism, but Hollywood paid little attention — yet — to what was taking place on the other side of the world.

The automobile business was evolving rapidly. Packard's Alvan Macauley had observed in 1933 that "there is not the quality, style, performance, or prestige differential between the low-priced car of today and a Packard that there was in 1925." Macauley's statement was even more true in 1939 than it had been six years earlier, for by that time even Chevrolet and Ford could boast 85 horsepower — 25 more than the Packard Six of 1925. Typical highway speeds had risen from 40 or so to 55 or even 60 miles an hour, and hydraulic brakes provided stopping power to match. Independent front suspension in most of the inexpensive cars had provided them with riding comfort that rivaled that of the limousines of an earlier generation. Styling clearly showed the influence of the classics. (Compare the lines of the 1939 Chevrolet, for example, with those of that year's Cadillac. And, of course, a major selling point of the medium-priced Packards was the fact that they looked almost exactly like the expensive "senior" cars that continued to be produced across the street.)

But the remarkable progress made by the industry in mass-producing fast, high-quality, moderately priced automobiles was only part of the story. Economics, too, played a role. During the depths of the Depression, when unemployment stood at record highs, coachbuilders and producers of what we now call "Classics" had been able to hire highly skilled labor for a virtual pittance. By decade's end, that would no longer be the case, and the painstaking hand work that went into the production of the cars of the Classic era would soon be beyond the reach of even the wealthiest citizens — if, indeed, such craftsmanship could be found at all.

1940 CADILLAC
BOHMAN & SCHWARTZ

Should this have been Cadillac's Continental?

THE thirties had passed into history, carrying with them one of the most creative periods of the twentieth century. War was on the horizon, a holocaust which changed the world, for better and for worse. After 1940 there would be no coachbuilding to speak of. There would be hot rods, and of course companies like Lehman-Peterson, specialists in limousine building on Cadillac or Lincoln chassis. But the days of the great coachbuilders were gone, swallowed up by an impatient world that didn't have time for hand-crafted work.

Art on wheels began to blossom in the mid-twenties when the wealthy wanted to arrive at their destination in a conversation piece rather than the boxy, practical designs favored by the car companies. Therefore, if you were rich,

by Nicky Wright
photos by the author

you headed for one of the specialty coachbuilders with your Cadillac, Packard or Locomobile chassis in tow.

Coachbuilders had been around ever since the motor car began. Many were well established builders to the carriage trade, so it was with little difficulty that the likes of The Derham Body Company converted to the business of making car bodies. Most of the early coachbuilders tended toward conservatism, most probably in the belief that the moneyed gentry preferred formal anonymity over "Hey, look, that's me!" ego trips.

Not so the gay young things (and I

don't mean gay in the current sense), the newly rich, Hollywood and the people so scathingly portrayed in F. Scott Fitzgerald's *The Great Gatsby.* As the twenties rolled into the thirties, new coachbuilders sprang up sporting exciting new talents completely at one with the prevailing winds of Art Deco, Salvador Dali, and Picasso. Liberated thoughts and expression flowed and blended the old world with the new. In America, particularly America, the art of palette and brush was translated in to sculpture, the sculpture of steel.

America's creative fervor came about in the worst possible time, smack bang in the middle of the worst economic depression the world had ever known. Yet it is at such times that art flows; arguably, perfect living standards such as in Sweden rarely produce good art. But

Originally published in Special Interest Autos #162, Nov.-Dec. 1997

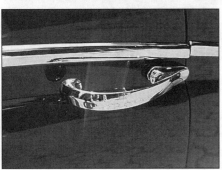

*Top left: Bohman & Schwartz coachbuilder tags are nearly hidden at bottom of cowl. **Above left:** Beautiful craftsmanship is seen in custom trim and door handles. **Above right:** Cadillac's "flying lady" mascot was retained in stock form. **Below:** Stock door sill plates also stayed.*

in Depression-torn America, art in all forms flourished, including the art of the coachbuilder.

At the beginning of the thirties, there were many great and expensive automobiles. There was Marmon, then Duesenberg, Cadillac, Stutz, Pierce-Arrow. All but one are gone now, driven to the wall by a combination of circumstances beginning with the Depression and ending with, in many cases, bad management. Not so Cadillac. The "Standard of the World" had General Motors behind it, to ensure Cadillac would never fail.

Dazzling coachbuilt bodies proliferated on the great marques during the early to mid-thirties. LeBaron, Murphy, Hibbard and Darrin, Willoughby, Weymann, Rollston, to name but a few, designed and built coachwork fit for a king . . . and in quite a few cases it was royalty who were the clients. Some designs were, of necessity, more formal

than others, but it was the radical and the rakish that caught Hollywood's eye.

Especially Bohman and Schwartz.

Bohman and Schwartz rose from the ashes of the great Walter M. Murphy Company of Pasadena, California. Beginning in August 1920 the coachbuilding talents of Murphy's company netted a heady list of patrons including kings, film stars, and socialites. In its short life span of 13 years, Murphy accounted for one third of all Duesenberg bodies, designed and built the fantastic Peerless V-16 prototype — the body was all aluminum, by the way — and pioneered the disappearing top. There were few shops finer than Murphy's to learn the art of coachbuilding.

Chris Bohman had been with Murphy from the beginning, and Maurice Schwartz, already a practiced body builder in his native Austria, joined in 1924 after a stint with Don Lee Coach-

works, Los Angeles, the shop where GM discovered Harley Earl. As the dark days of perpetual winter descended upon Murphy, Bohman and Schwartz, realizing there were customers' cars yet to be completed, made a bid to finish the work. Their offer was accepted by grateful clients who were more than satisfied with the results. Other work was in the offing, so the two men hired other ex-Murphy employees and set up in the business of coachbuilding as Bohman and Schwartz, first at DeLacey and Green Streets, then at 326 W. Colorado Street, Pasadena.

From the very beginning, Bohman and Schwartz caught the eye of the public. Their designs owed nothing to anyone else, nor were they meant to. Car design had become an art form, and Bohman and Schwartz rapidly became the style leaders of the mid to late thirties. Take some of the Duesenbergs for example.

1940 Cadillac

Flowing, low lines, high waists and fender skirts became a trademark, so much so that Prince Serge M'Divani ordered one. So did Henry Topping, Jr., and Ethel V. Mars of Mars candy bar fame had an incredible SJ Town Car that was as different as a Matisse painting.

Soon, Bohman and Schwartz's order book read like a Who's Who of the world. Many others of the rich and famous brought their existing cars to Bohman

and Schwartz and commissioned new bodies. Clark Gable was one. He took his Rollston-designed JN convertible to the Pasadena company for a complete restyling job. And in 1937 Bohman and Schwartz undertook to build Rust Heinz, of Heinz Soups, his futuristic Phantom Corsair (see *SIA* #17) out of the young Heinz's Cord sedan.

Ever since Cadillac won two Dewar Trophies for standardization of parts and the self starter and proclaimed itself the "Standard of the World," the marque rose through the ranks to become the undisputed luxury car leader in Amer-

ica. Not that that was difficult. Apart from Lincoln who only now is beginning to erode Cadillac's leadership, all other US luxury car contenders have disappeared into oblivion.

To enhance its growing reputation as leader, Cadillac offered V-12 and V-16 engines and perhaps because it built more cars than any other luxury maker, relied almost exclusively on coachwork by Fleetwood and Fisher, both concerns belonging to GM, who handed Fleetwood to Cadillac. It was a rare sight indeed to see a Cadillac with coachwork by an outside company. Vanden Plas, Brunn,

specifications

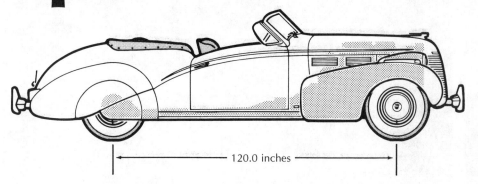

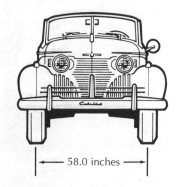

← 120.0 inches →

← 58.0 inches →

1940 Cadillac Bohman & Schwartz convertible

ENGINE
Type	L-head, 90-degree V-8, water-cooled, cast en bloc, 3 mains, full pressure lubrication, cast-iron heads.
Bore x stroke	3.50 inches x 4.50 inches
Displacement	346 cubic inches
Compression ratio	6.25:1
Max. bhp @ rpm	135 @ 3.400
Max. torque @ rpm	250 @ 1,700
Induction system	Stromberg 2-bbl. downdraft carb, mechanical fuel pump.
Exhaust system	Cast-iron manifolds, crossover pipe at top rear of block, single exhaust and muffler
Electrical system	6-volt battery/coil (Delco-Remy)

CLUTCH
Type	Single dry plate, Long semi-centrifugal, woven asbestos lining
Diameter	10.5 inches
Actuation	Mechanical, foot pedal

TRANSMISSION
Type	3-speed manual, column lever, synchro on 2nd and high.
Ratios: 1st	2.39:1
2nd	1.53:1
3rd	1.00:1
Reverse	2.39:1

DIFFERENTIAL
Type	Hotchkiss, hypoid, spiral-bevel gears.
Ratio	3.92:1
Drive axles	Semi-floating

STEERING
Type	Worm and roller (Saginaw)
Turns lock-to-lock	4.1
Ratio	19:1
Turn circle	46.0 feet

BRAKES
Type	Hydraulic, 4-wheel drums, internal expanding (Bendix).
Drum diameter	12.0 inches
Total swept area	208.0 square inches

CHASSIS & BODY
Frame	Channel-section steel, double-dropped, central I-beam X-member
Body	Steel, bolted to frame, cloth top (Fisher).
Body style	5-passenger, 4-door convertible sedan, manual top

SUSPENSION
Front	Unequal-length independent A-arms, coil springs. Delco lever shocks, cross-link stabilizer bar.
Rear	Solid axle, longitudinal leaf springs, lever shocks, cross-link stabilizer bar.
Tires	7.00 x 16 4-ply tube type
Wheels	Pressed steel, bolt-ons, drop-center rims.

WEIGHTS AND MEASURES
Wheelbase	120.0 inches
Overall length	215.8 inches
Overall width	75.6 inches
Overall height	65.3 inches
Front track	58.0 inches
Rear track	59.0 inches
Ground clearance	9.6 inches
Curb weight	4,230 pounds

FUEL CONSUMPTION
Average	12-14 mpg

Facing page, top: Imposing Caddy grille treatment has some Cord 810 influence. *Below left:* Squared-off front fenders give a semi-formal appearance. *Center right:* But rear fenders are much more dashing. *Below right:* Coachline carried through into cutaway fender skirt gives a European appearance. *This page:* This is a car that looks right with wide whitewalls.

1940 Cadillac

continued

Above: There's a dazzling amount of chrome on the windshield frame and on the dashboard. Below: When new, car had auxiliary road lights.

courtesy of Michael Lamm

Franay of Paris, and Derham all tried their hand, not always with Cadillac's blessing, but it was Bohman and Schwartz who ended up making one of the most interesting designs on a Cadillac chassis.

By 1940 coachbuilding was becoming a lost art. Few remained to carry on a great tradition begun almost half a century before. Many great companies were lost to the Depression, others died because there was less work around. War was raging across the globe, and it was only a matter of time before America would be forced to join in.

There wasn't much for Bohman and Schwartz to do. What designs they did heralded a new era, the era of extrovert styling that emerged during the fifties when customizer George Barris was king. Perhaps W. Everett Miller the designer, Bohman and Schwartz the builders, foresaw this coming trend when they custom-built two 1940 Cadillac convertible coupes on spec.

Miller's design layouts for the Cadillac so intrigued Bohman and Schwartz that they decided to go out on a limb and build it. An order for the car would have been nice, but rather like fashion designers, the partners hoped what they built would wow enough people to want to buy them. In the event they would have to attract enough to buy two identical models....

Cadillac made 1,322 coupes on the new 129-inch-wheelbase Series 62 that appeared for the first time in 1940. Featuring all-new styling in 1938, Cadillacs were facelifted in 1939, then again in 1940. A 1940 standout was the bolder grille, twin vents on each side of the hood, and larger taillights.

Multi-cylinder power had all but gone in 1940; only the Lincoln had 12 cylinders and Cadillac tried one more year with its second generation V-16. As for the Series 62, it was equipped with the 342-cubic-inch, 135-horse side-valve V-8, regarded by many as one of the best engines of its day. It was the Series 62 coupe that Bohman and Schwartz chose to give their highly individual treatment.

What resulted is on these pages. From the grille to the windshield is unmistakably Cadillac. From the rakish cast bronze windshield back is nothing Cadillac would have produced at the factory. Note the chrome molding following a pronounced curve along the cut-down doors, almost to the rear fender and above it, an early example of the pinched waist look that was later to be used extensively by Harley Earl during the fifties. Whether he got the idea from the Bohman and Schwartz Cadillac is not known, though it is doubtful.

Above the dashboard, which is stock Cadillac, there is a leather-covered pad-

ded roll which extends across the tops of the doors. The interior is rich with somewhat ostentatious cream leather, but the front bucket seats are well before their time. At the rear, a shortened trunk gives this custom Cadillac the long-hood, short-deck look of an elegant Grand Tourer.

Perhaps it was the uncertain times. Perhaps the two identical Bohman and Schwartz Cadillacs were too radical. Or was it the fact that the new, redesigned 1941 Cadillacs were already in the showrooms? Whatever the reason, Bohman and Schwartz could not get rid of the pair. Eventually, both were finally sold, the one shown here going to William Doheny, the controversial president of Sinclair Oil who was indicted on bribery and conspiracy charges with his boss, Harry Sinclair. They were questionably acquitted after long and protracted litigation.

Several years later Doheny, who was friendly with Bohman and Schwartz, invited Chris Bohman to a party at his elaborate, castle-like mansion in Beverly Hills. Desperate to sell the Cadillacs,

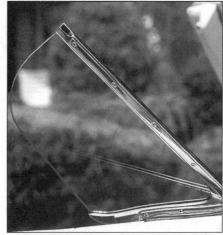

Above left: Sumptuous leather interior coddles driver and passengers. ***Above right:*** *Windwings were another B&S custom touch.* ***Below left:*** *Wonderfully smooth and quiet 346 flathead V-8 complements smooth looks of the car.* ***Below right:*** *Rear seat access is convenient.* ***Bottom:*** *Interior treatment is somewhat Darrinesque; gives feeling of low-slung cockpit.*

Chris Bohman drove one to the party. According to designer Strother MacMinn, the Doheny family, including his daughter and son-in-law, came out to admire the car. While Chris Bohman was showing off the car, Doheny's daughter's dog jumped into the car and "sat down between the two bucket seats. And that," wrote MacMinn, "clinched the deal."

I am not sure what happened to the second car, but we are able to follow the Doheny car to its present owner. The Cadillac remained in the Doheny family for several years before it eventually made its way to Washington, D.C., and the second owner, in 1976.

When Terry Radey of Toronto, Ontario, Canada, found the car and bought it in 1984, it was a real basket case. Terry handed the car over to Georgetown, Ontario, restorer Nick Rampling, who after much research and many, many hours of painstaking work, brought the car back to the condition you see here. "He [Rampling] is a true artisan and the real hero in the story," says Radey with much pride.

A ride around the suburbs of Toronto speaks highly of Rampling's meticulous work, for the Cadillac is as good, if not better, than it was the day Chris Bohman originally sold it to Doheny. Driving effortlessly along on a late, warm summer's evening, one is reminded of a different world long gone, of bespoke tailoring that quietly whispered class. Many have recognized the grace and elegance of Terry Radey's Cadillac, as can be attested by the awards, including the 1991 Chairman's Choice at the Meadowbrook Concours, and the 1992 Journalist's Award at the Burn Foundation Concours.

Chris Bohman and Maurice Schwartz dissolved their partnership in 1947 and went their separate ways. Bohman passed away sometime before Schwartz, who continued to build fancy bodywork for many clients, including the late William Harrah. In March 1961, Maurice Schwartz died at the age of 76.

Artists may die, but their art lives on as their gift to the rest of us. We are able to learn and to appreciate the finer things of life because of great painters, great writers, great film makers.

And great coachbuilders like Bohman and Schwartz. ෨

1941 Cadillac Series 63
The Last LaSalle

by Arch Brown
photos by Bud Juneau

NINETEEN forty-one was a banner year for the 38-year-old Cadillac Motor Car Division. Calendar year production totalled 59,572 vehicles, shattering the previous all-time record of 41,172 units, set back in 1928. Perhaps surprisingly, the new record—unlike that of 1928—was established without the help of the LaSalle, Cadillac's high-styled but slightly less costly "companion" car.

Management had taken a gamble in dropping the LaSalle at the end of the 1940 model run, for, especially in recent times, it had consistently outsold the Cadillac. Consider the production figures for the final eight years of the LaSalle's lifespan:

	Cadillac	LaSalle
1933	3,173	3,482
1934	5,819	7,195
1935	3,636	8,651
1936	12,880	13,004
1937	14,152	32,000
1938	9,375	15,575
1939	13,581	22,001
1940	13,046	24,130

Surely there must have been those in the corporate board room who counseled caution, for General Motors has never been one to mess with success. And after all, 1940 had been the second-best year in history for the LaSalle, with sales running 85 percent ahead of Cadillac's. On the face of it, to cease production of a popular and highly respected automobile, almost at the pinnacle of its success, must have appeared to many people to be an act of sheer folly.

But the lesson of the Packard One-Twenty had not been lost upon the men of Cadillac. In 1935 the proud Packard Motor Car Company had introduced the medium-priced Packard One-Twenty, and from Day One its sales had outstripped those of the LaSalle. In fact, over the six-year period 1935-1940, inclusive, The One-Twenty's sales volume had averaged 72 percent greater than that of its counterpart from Cadillac.

The message, then, was clear enough. Since the LaSalle was to all intents and

purposes a Cadillac in all but name (and had been so throughout its lifespan, except for 1934-36, when Cadillac had raided the Oldsmobile parts bin in order

Instead of Cadillac's traditional crest on the front and rear, the 63 may have ended up with LaSalle's handsome script and that family's coat of arms if decisions at the division had been different.

to produce a cheaper LaSalle), it was time to bestow upon it the prestigious Cadillac title.

The decision to drop the LaSalle was evidently made almost at the last minute, by which time several styling proposals had been made for a 1941 model. At least three wood-and-metal mock-ups were built. (Strictly speaking they were not prototypes, for they had

no running gear.) In contrast to the massive, horizontal bridgework that would be introduced on the production '41 Cadillacs, all three LaSalle proposals carried forward the tall, narrow, vertical grille that had been a LaSalle characteristic since 1934.

The first of these mock-ups had a pronounced rear deck. In reality it was a carry-over of the "C"-body used for the 1940 LaSalle Series 52 as well as the Cadillac Series 62 and senior models of Buick, Oldsmobile, and even Pontiac. The second was a fastback which would become the sensational new 1941 GM "B" body; while the third was a modified notchback, derived from the fastback but provided with a modest "bustle," much less prominent than that of the "C" body.

It was the third rendition that became the body of the Cadillac Series 63 of 1941-42, just as the fastback "B" body was used for the Series 61 and the extended-deck "C" body for the Series 62.

Inevitably, there have been questions, over the years:
• If this modified notchback design was originally intended for a 1941 LaSalle, Cadillac's least expensive car, how come it ended up on a pricier model than either the Sixty-One or the Sixty-Two?
• Might this styling have been originally intended as the *only* LaSalle series? There would have been a certain logic to this, for as recently as 1939 there had been just one LaSalle, sharing in that instance the "B" body of the smaller Buicks and the larger Oldsmobiles and Pontiacs.
• Or could the company have been thinking of producing three LaSalles, presumably titled the Series 51, 52 and 53, employing all three design proposals? Mock-ups of all of them had been developed, after all. • Why was this body used exclusively by Cadillac? It certainly would have made an attractive Buick, for example. • And why was it produced only in sedan form, particularly at a time when the club

Originally published in Special Interest Autos #159, May.-June 1997

coupe was enjoying increasing popularity?

Bud Juneau, who, in addition to his widely recognized photographic expertise, serves as editor of the Cadillac-LaSalle Club's annual publication, *The Self-Starter*, set about to find the answer to at least some of these questions. Among the Cadillac experts that Bud interviewed was long-time General Motors stylist Dave Holls.

Juneau: "In your conversations with [GM Chief Stylist] Bill Mitchell, did you ever get the impression that the Series 63 body had been intended for the LaSalle?"

Holls: "I asked Bill about the 63 series, because it seemed strange that this body would be placed above the 61 and 62, since in the rest of GM, this sort of six window configuration was the bottom of the line. The

streamlined fastback was next, and the notch back was top in such cars as Buick, Olds and Pontiac. This thing was sort of an 'A' body, not quite a notch back and not quite a deck. Bill inferred that this was going to be the LaSalle for 1941. This would make sense, with it at

This styling mockup from 1939 shows the projected 1941 LaSalle using the body that the Cadillac 63 used after LaSalle was discontinued. These bodies may have been in production by the time LaSalle was dropped; so a new series of Cadillac was invented to use them up. This rather attractive body was not shared with other divisions.

the bottom of the line, the B body fastback being the next step up, the first level Cadillac, and the C body as the 62 series."

Juneau: "Did you get the impression that it was going to be for the exclusive use of LaSalle?

Holls: "All he said was that the body was going to be used for the LaSalle. I don't recall the use of the word exclusively, and he didn't say if it was going to be shared anywhere else. It would be a logical assumption that by the time the decision was made to drop LaSalle, the body was too far along in production to be scrapped, so they went ahead and made the Cadillac 63. I can't say if they were planning to make both all along, except that it's the usual policy to share bodies."

All of which, if it answers one question, serves also to raise another: Once the decision was made to go forward

*Above: True "eggcrate" grille theme began in '41. **Below:** More Caddy crests on hood accents and fender skirts. DriveReport car carries factory accessory fog lights. **Facing page, top:** Eggcrate theme continues on hood sides. **Center:** Discreet window trim provides nice finishing touch. **Bottom:** Bars on rear window add touch of formality.*

1941 Cadillac

with this body, why was it exclusive to Cadillac? As Dave Holls indicated, it was (and remains) General Motors' policy to share body shells among the various divisions, thus keeping unit costs to a minimum.

These questions must, of course, go unanswered, for the men who were in charge at Cadillac, back in 1941—Chief

Designer William Mitchell, for example, and General Manager Nicholas Dreystadt—are all deceased now. All we know is what actually took place as the 1941 model year opened. • With the LaSalle out of the picture, the new Series 61 became Cadillac's entry-level car. Built on a wheelbase of 126 inches, three inches longer than either of the two 1940 LaSalle series (but an inch shorter than the 1940 Series 62 Cadillac), it weighed anywhere from 130 to 285 pounds more than its immediate predecessors. And at $1,345 for the

fastback five-passenger coupe, the best-selling model in the entire Cadillac line, it actually cost $35.00 less than the 1940 LaSalle "52" coupe. Not since the one-cylinder models of 1908 had any Cadillac carried such a reasonable price tag. • Retained for a second year was the bustle-back Cadillac Series 62. A drastic $250 price cut positioned this popular car just $50.00 above the Series 61. We hasten to add, however, that these prices, for both the "61" and "62" series, were for standard models. For a premium of about $90.00 the buyer of either of them could opt for deluxe equipment, which included an upgraded interior with Bedford cord upholstery and some additional bright trim, as well as fender skirts, which Cadillac called "wheel shields."

And then there was the Series 63, our featured car. Its body shell, though derived from the General Motors "B" body (with which doors and fenders were interchangeable), was exclusive to Cadillac. It was offered only as a deluxe-trimmed four-door touring sedan, and it was obviously intended as a premium model, offering the buyer something exclusive for $161 (10.5 percent) more than the price of a Series 62 Deluxe sedan.

It is this car, it seems to us, that could be thought of as "the almost-forgotten Cadillac." For it appears that any number of car buffs either have never heard of it, or fail to remember that it was ever produced. Perhaps this isn't all that surprising, for the "63" was not a high-volume line. Only 5,050 of these fine cars were built for the 1941 model run,

followed by 1,740 examples turned out during the abbreviated 1942 season, after which it was dropped from the line. One is left to wonder whether General Motors could have even recouped its tooling costs from a total, two-year production of 6,790 cars.

If the body of the Series 63 was distinctive, or at least exclusive to Cadillac, its engine was nothing new. Developed under the leadership, first of Owen Nacker, and later of Jack Gordon, who would later become president of General Motors, it was first introduced in 1936. This V-8 represented a major advance in engine construction, for it featured a single-unit, cast iron block, replacing the three-piece construction which had been in use since Cadillac introduced the V-8 in 1914. At least equally importantly, this was the first Cadillac L-head engine to employ hydraulic valve lash adjusters.

Two versions of this engine were offered during the introductory year. The smaller of the two, displacing 322.2

cubic inches and rated at 125 horse-power, was used, initially, to power the Series 60, the car that took Cadillac into the upper-medium price field, and from 1937 through 1940 it was fitted to the LaSalle.

The other new engine, employed by the larger eight-cylinder Cadillacs during 1936 and throughout the line thereafter, was simply a bored version of the "322" block, with a displacement of 346.4 cubes. Output was rated at 135 horsepower initially, though in 1941 an increase in the compression ratio from 6.25:1 to 7.25:1 boosted that figure to 150 bhp. It was this seemingly indestructible V-8 that powered the Army's M-5 and M-24 tanks and the M-8 Howitzer Motor Carriage during World War II, and went on to serve as Cadillac's "work horse" through the 1948 model year.

Mechanically, the Series 63 was identical to the "61," the "62" and even the Fleetwood Sixty-Special. Heading the list of Cadillac engineering innovations for 1941 was the HydraMatic transmis-

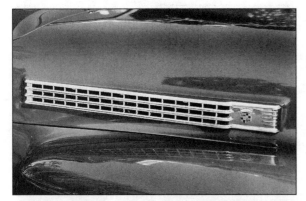

1941 Cadillac Prices, Weights and Production

Series/body type	Price	Weight	Production
Series 61, 126-inch wheelbase			
Coupe (fastback)	$1,345	3,985	11,812
Deluxe coupe (fastback)	1,435	4,005	3,015
Sedan	1,445	4,065	10,925
Deluxe sedan	1,535	4,085	3,495
Chassis	n/a	n/a	
Series 62, 126-inch wheelbase			
Coupe	1,420	3,950	1,985
Deluxe coupe	1,510	3,970	1,900
Sedan	1,495	4,030	8,012
Deluxe sedan	1,535	4,050	7,754
Convertible coupe	1,645	4,055	3,100
Convertible sedan	1,965	4,230	400
Chassis	n/a	n/a	4
Series 63, 126-inch wheelbase			
Touring sedan	1,695	4,140	5,050
Fleetwood Series 60-Special, 126-inch wheelbase			
Sedan	2,195	4,230	3,693
Sedan, sun roof	n/a	n/a	185
Imperial sedan	2,345	4,290	220
Town car	n/a	n/a	1
Chassis	n/a	n/a	1
Series 67, 139-inch wheelbase			
Sedan, 5-passenger	2,595	4,230	315
Sedan, 7-passenger	2,735	4,630	280
Imperial sedan, 5-passenger	2,745	4,615	95
Imperial sedan, 7-passenger	2,890	4.705	210
Fleetwood Series 75, 136-inch wheelbase			
Business sedan, 9-passenger	2,895	4,750	54
Business Imperial, 9-passenger	3,050	4,810	8
Sedan, 5-passenger	2,995	4,750	422
Sedan, 7-passenger	3,140	4,800	405
Imperial sedan, 5-passenger	3,150	4,810	132
Imperial sedan, 7-passenger	3,295	4,860	757
Formal sedan, 5-passenger	3,920	4,900	75
Formal sedan, 7-passenger	4,045	4,915	98
Chassis	n/a	n/a	5
Commercial chassis, 163-inch wheelbase	n/a	n/a	150

specifications

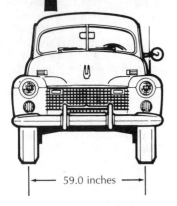

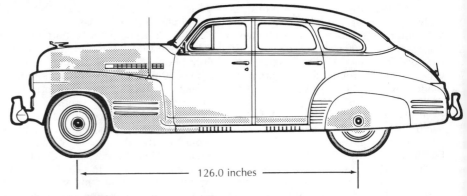

← 59.0 inches →

← 126.0 inches →

1941 Cadillac Sixty-Three

Original price	$1,695 f.o.b. factory, with standard equipment
Std. equip. this model	Fender skirts, clock, rear center armrest, ash tray and lighter
Options on dR car	Radio with vacuum-operated antenna, white sidewall tires, twin front under-seat heater/ defrosters, fog lights, backup lights

ENGINE

Type	L-head V-8
Bore x stroke	3.5 inches x 4.5 inches
Displacement	346.0 cubic inches
Compression ratio	7.25:1
Horsepower @ rpm	150 @ 3,400
Torque @ rpm	283 @ 1,700
Taxable horsepower	39.2
Valve lifters	Hydraulic
Main bearings	3
Carburetor	Dual downdraft
Lubrication system	Pressure
Cooling system	Centrifugal pump
Exhaust system	Single
Electrical system	Delco-Remy 6-volt battery/coil

TRANSMISSION

Type	3-speed selective, synchronized 2nd and 3rd gears, column-mounted control
Ratios: 1st	2.39:1
2nd	1.53:1
3rd	1.00:1
Reverse	2.39:1

CLUTCH

Type	Single dry plate
Diameter	10.5 inches
Actuation	Mechanical, foot pedal

DIFFERENTIAL

Type	Hypoid
Ratio	3.36:1
Drive axles	Semi-floating

STEERING

Type	Worm and nut
Turns lock-to-lock	5
Gear ratio	23.6:1
Turning diameter	38 feet 2 inches (curb/curb)

BRAKES

Type	4-wheel hydraulic, drum type
Drum diameter	12 inches
Effective area	208 square inches

CHASSIS & BODY

Construction	Body-on-frame
Frame	U-section steel, double-dropped, central X-member
Body construction	All steel
Body type	4-door touring sedan

SUSPENSION

Front	Independent, coil springs
Rear	Rigid axle, 54.5-inch x 2-inch 8-leaf semi-elliptic springs
Shock absorbers	Two-way lever type
Tires	7.00/15 4-ply
Wheels	Pressed steel disc

WEIGHTS AND MEASURES

Wheelbase	126 inches
Overall length	215 inches
Overall width	80 inches
Overall height	64.5 inches
Front track	59 inches
Rear track	63 inches
Min. road clearance	8 inches
Shipping weight	4,140 pounds

CAPACITIES

Crankcase	7 quarts
Cooling system	25 quarts
Fuel tank	20 gallons
Transmission	2.5 pounds
Rear axle	5 pounds

CALCULATED DATA

Stroke/bore ratio	1.286:1
Horsepower per c.i.d.	.430
Weight per hp	27.6 pounds
Weight per c.i.d.	12.0 pounds
P.S.I. (brakes)	19.9
Crankshaft revs/mile	2,748
Production, this series/ body type	5,050

PERFORMANCE

Top speed	95.2 mph
Fuel mileage	15.3 mpg

From General Motors Proving Ground test, 5/12/51

---

*Headlamps and fog lights work harmoniously into front fender design. **Far right:** Plate lamp/trunk handle echoes sharpness of car's styling.*

1941 Cadillac

sion, a $125 option, introduced by the Oldsmobile Division a year earlier. Not a few motorists were dubious about this fully automatic, four-speed gearbox at first, for it was something radically new. But — fitted to military vehicles in combination with the Cadillac engine — it would go on to deliver outstanding service under the most difficult of wartime conditions.

All of which is perhaps beside the point, for some 70 percent of all 1941 Cadillacs, including our feature car, were delivered with the three-speed standard transmission, an excellent gearbox, and incidentally a favorite with hot-rodders everywhere because of its well-chosen ratios and smooth action — not to mention its stout construction.

Driving Impressions

Bob Briggs, recently retired director of the University of California's famous band, had always been intrigued by the Cadillac 63, and three years ago he set about to see whether one might be available. Remarkably, considering their relative scarcity, he found four examples advertised. Following up on the ads, he learned that one had already been sold. He got no response from the second owner, but he was able to make detailed inquiries about the other cars. Of the two, the one that seemed to be the more promising was located in Pennsylvania; so Bob flew there, inspected the automobile, bought it on the spot and had it shipped to California.

The Cadillac, which had logged about 74,000 miles when Briggs bought it, had had just two prior owners, the second one having purchased it from the estate of the first. The original buyer, who had owned it throughout most of its lifespan, was a Massachusetts lady, and the car had been driven and maintained by her chauffeur. (In fact, when the Cad arrived in California, Bob found a chauffeur's cap and a lady's parasol in the back seat.)

Bob Briggs is not one to let his collector cars sit idle. He has added another 23,000 miles to the Cadillac's odometer. For touring purposes, Bob built a shelf in the trunk, below which his tools are stored. Even with the shelf in place, there is adequate space for luggage. In 1995 Briggs drove to Rapid City, South Dakota, where he joined up with the Classic Car Club for the final leg of its Coast-to-Coast Caravan. The Cadillac, he reports, performed flawlessly, one flat tire being the only problem he encountered.

There was, however, some bearing noise by the time Bob got home; so he pulled the pan to have a look at the sit-

Top and bottom: For a two-tons-plus car the Caddy holds the road very well indeed. Below: This was the first year for the trick gas cap on Caddys.

uation. There were piston fragments in the pan, so it was obvious that the engine needed to be rebuilt. It was sent to Moose Motors, of Penngrove, California, for that purpose.

One thing tends to lead to another, as every car hobbyist knows. With the engine out, it was easy to paint the firewall; so why not paint the entire automobile? Understandably, the original black paint was not in the best of shape; so Briggs, after consulting the 1941 Cadillac color chart, sent the car to Nelson Brooks, of Byron, California, where it was refinished in Berkshire Green over Cimarron Green. (Bob tells

us that this was the only authentic 1941 two-tone combination in which the darker color was used for the top.) Rechroming by the Walkers' shop in Vacaville completed the cosmetic restoration; for the car's interior is original, and in remarkably good condition.

As we slipped into the Cadillac for our test drive, we spotted a little body plate that explains a lot, it seems to us, about the Series 63. It reads, "Body by Fisher, Interior by Fleetwood." It is really a lovely, high-quality automobile.

And a fine driver! Thanks to those hydraulic valve lash adjusters, the engine runs quietly. This particular car is

equipped with the 3.36:1 axle normally found in combination with the HydraMatic transmission, in place of the customary 3.77:1 cogs. As a result, the engine almost literally loafs at freeway speeds, though of course this comes at some small sacrifice in off-the-line performance as well as

1941 Cadillac

*Above: Lots of chrome inside, too. **Top right:** Radiator's thermostatic shutter control. **Right:** Heating system is controlled solely by driver. **Facing page, top left:** Delicately designed overhead light. **Center:** 63 had Fleetwood interior standard. **Top right:** Faithful, tough 346 flathead carried on proud V-8 tradition. **Below left:** Car's original chauffeur's cap and owner's parasol. **Right:** Understated, yet thoroughly modern for '41.*

A Little Something Extra
The Cadillac 63 and The Chrysler Crown Imperial Compared

Cadillac's volume lines during 1941 were the Series 61 and 62, while the best-selling eight-cylinder Chryslers were the Saratoga and New Yorker models. In each instance, however, the manufacturer had something to offer the motorist who wanted a more exclusive version, and didn't mind paying a premium price. Hence, the Cadillac "63" Sedan and the Chrysler Crown Imperial Town Sedan. Neither car was produced in great volume. The Imperial, especially, is very rare, for it was introduced at mid-season, and it disappeared at the end of the 1941 model run after just 894 examples had been produced. But it was a very attractive car, beautifully trimmed and distinguished by blind quarter panels — a worthy competitor for the Cadillac 63.

Here's how these two premium-level cars compared:

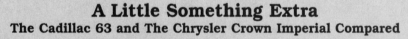

	Cadillac 63	Crown Imperial
Original price	$1,696	$1,760
Wheelbase	126 inches	127.5 inches
Overall length	215 inches	217.8125 inches
Overall width	80 inches	77.75 inches
Shipping weight (lb.)	4,140	3,900
Track, front/rear	59 inches/63 inches	58 inches/62 inches
Engine	V-8	Straight 8
Bore x stroke	3.5 inches x 4.5 inches	3.25 inches x 4.875 inches
Displacement (cu. in.)	346.0	323.5
Compression ratio	7.25:1	6.80:1
Horsepower @ rpm	150 @ 3,400 rpm	140 @ 3,400
Torque @ rpm	283 @ 1,700	260/1,600
Automatic trans. (opt.)	HydraMatic	Vacamatic (semi-auto)
Standard axle ratio	3.77:1	3.91:1
Steering	Worm & nut	Worm & roller
Braking area (sq. in.)	208.0	189.2
Tire size	7.00/15	7.00/15
Stroke/bore ratio	1.286:1	1.500:1
Horsepower per c.i.d.	.430	.433
Weight (lb.) per hp	27.6	27.9
Crankshaft revs per mile	2,748	2,850

Notes:

1. Cadillac charged $125 extra for the HydraMatic transmission during 1941.

2. Fluid Drive was standard equipment on the Imperial, but the semi-automatic M-3 "Vacamatic" cost extra.

3. Crankshaft revs per mile were computed using standard axle ratios.

4. The Chrysler Imperial Town Sedan was the only 1941 Imperial to be built on the 127.5-inch C-30 chassis of the New Yorker. All other models came on a 145.5-inch wheelbase.

hill-climbing ability. (A good trade, in our view.)

Steering is fairly precise; and while it couldn't be called light, it's not as heavy as one might expect of a non-powered unit in a relatively heavy car. Brakes, by 1941 standards, are among the best. Clutch action is smooth and pedal pressure is light; and the transmission shifts easily and crisply.

Seats are comfortable and supportive. Leg room is more than adequate, both front and rear; and the ride rivals the best of modern automobiles. Acceleration, despite the numerically low axle ratio, is quite good for a car of this era. No doubt a '41 Buick Century, equipped with compound carburetion, would take it handily in a drag race, and a Packard One-Sixty might enjoy a slight edge, but most other 1941 cars would struggle to keep up with the Cadillac.

We're still mystified by the fact that the car that was originally intended to be a LaSalle ended up outranking both the Cadillac Sixty-One and Sixty-Two. But however that came about, the result is an automobile that is both attractive and distinctive. ॐ

Acknowledgments and Bibliography

Bell, James D, "The Cadillac Standard," Automobile Quarterly, Vol. III, No. 3; Hendry, Maurice D, Cadillac, The Complete History; Juneau, Bud (ed.), 1991 Self-Starter Annual; Kimes, Beverly Rae and Henry Austin Clark, Jr., Standard Catalog of US Cars, 1805-1942; McCall, Walter M.P., 80 Years of Cadillac/LaSalle.

Our thanks to The Alan Short Gallery, Stockton, California, which supplied the setting for Bud Juneau's photo session. Special thanks to Bob Briggs, Fairfield, California.

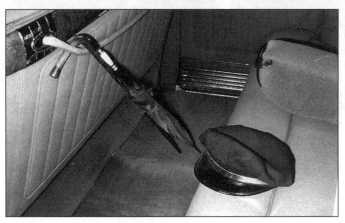

1941

Nineteen forty-one: One of the most critical years in American history. In the world's history, for that matter. Each day brought our nation a step or two closer to full participation in the war that had raged in Europe since 1939.

On March 10th, President Roosevelt signed the seven billion dollar Lend-Lease Act, without which Britain would surely have fallen, leaving the United States to face the Nazi menace virtually alone. A month later the Office of Price Administration was established in an effort to keep a lid on prices. On June 14th, assets of Germany and Italy in this country were frozen, ships of German and Italian registry in U.S. ports were seized, and German consulates were closed. And on July 6th, the President brought the need for our participation in the rapidly expanding conflict into sharp focus by enunciating four principles of human liberty, known collectively as the "Four Freedoms": Freedom of speech and expression, freedom of worship, freedom from want, and freedom from fear.

It happened that while all this was going on, this writer was a junior at the University of California. A favorite student watering hole, in those days, was a German beer garden in San Francisco. The beer was excellent, and cheap; and an old-fashioned German band provided the

accompaniment for traditional German dances. As I recall, the "cover" charge was twenty-five cents per person. Like students everywhere, we were always on the lookout for bargains, and the beer garden provided an evening of great entertainment for very little money.

And then, one day without warning, the beer garden was closed, and we were told that it had been a "front" for the pro-Nazi German-American Bund. In short, the place was a haven for German spies.

It's safe to say that most Americans, students included, had not yet come to fully realize the gravity of the world situation. Serious-minded readers were immersed in William L. Shirer's *Berlin Diary*, but most people opted for such works of fiction as A. J. Cronin's *The Keys of the Kingdom* and J. P. Marquand's *H. M. Pulham, Esq.* At the movies, along with the World War I saga *Sergeant York*, starring Gary Cooper, we saw Monty Woolley in *The Man Who Came to Dinner*, Walter Pidgeon in *How Green Was My Valley*, and *Citizen Kane*, starring Orson Welles. Ann Sheridan and Robert Cummings played the leading roles in *Kings Row*, with Ronald Reagan in a minor but memorable part.

The tendency of so many people to prefer escapism to reality was equally apparent in much of the popular music of the day. Major hits included "Chattanooga Choo

Choo," "Blues In the Night," "I Got It Bad and That Ain't Good," "Jersey Bounce," and "Deep In the Heart of Texas." But a few songs reflected the realities of the world situation. "The White Cliffs of Dover," for instance, poignantly expressed England's hope for a peaceful world to come; and "I Don't Want to Walk Without You" gave a hint of the anxiety and the loneliness of young lovers separated by the military draft.

Still, there was a bright side. The New York Yankees beat the Brooklyn Dodgers 4-1 to win the World Series; while Yankee center fielder Joe DiMaggio set a record by hitting safely in 56 games.

And then, on December 7th—the day after President Roosevelt addressed a personal appeal to Emperor Hirohito to avoid further conflict in the Pacific—America was suddenly, rudely awakened. The illusion of peace was abruptly shattered by the Japanese attack on Pearl Harbor, followed quickly by attacks upon Guam, Wake Island and the Philippines. We were at war! Thousands of lives would be lost, and countless thousands of others irrevocably changed, as America shouldered the unaccustomed responsibility of the military as well as the political leadership of the world.

And in Detroit, automobile production was halted "for the duration."

SIA comparisonReport

1941 Cadillac Sixty-Two and Packard One-Sixty

by Arch Brown
photos by Jim Tanji

THE WHISTLES blew and the sirens wailed, marking the beginning of what was to be a fateful year: 1941. In Washington, Franklin D. Roosevelt was about to be inaugurated for an unprecedented third term as president of the United States. Overseas, France had fallen before the advancing German armies, and England stood alone as democracy's last strategic bastion in Europe. Unable to bomb the British into submission, Hitler was busy making plans to invade the Soviet Union. And on the other side of the globe the Japanese, stalemated in their attempt to take over China, prepared for a war of conquest in the Pacific.

Meanwhile, America slept.

Technically, of course, the United States was at peace. A military draft had been instituted, and US Naval vessels were being prepared for convoy duty, ferrying war materiel to the beleaguered British. But apart from harmless training exercises, our men had not yet taken up arms—and most Americans confidently expected to keep it that way. Before the year was out, that illusion would be dispelled.

The Depression was at long last over. Fueled by war-related orders, the econ-

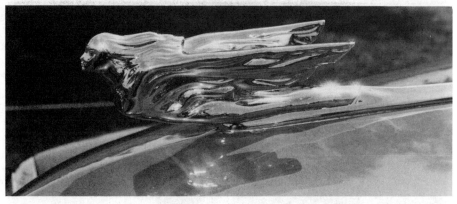

omy was booming once more, and Americans were going back to work. They were also buying automobiles—more of them than at any time in nearly a dozen years. And more expensive ones, as well. It's not just that the prices of the "low-priced three" had risen twice as fast as those of the medium-priced makes—though in fact they had, narrowing the gap between Chevrolet and Buick, for instance, to as little as $200. But whereas in 1934 Chevrolet, Ford and Plymouth among them accounted for nearly three-quarters of what little new-car market there was, by 1941 their collective share had slipped to just over half the total. True, their production was running nearly 28 percent ahead of what it had been seven years earlier, but over the same period the big three of the medium-price field—Buick, Olds and Chrysler—had increased their combined output by an astonishing 248 percent!

But there was yet another dimension to the story.

Correctly sensing that the day of the ultra-high-priced luxury automobile was nearly over, Cadillac had created, in 1936, a whole new genre with its Sixty series (see SIA #69). By employing the Cadillac engine and drivetrain, fitted with the body and assorted other components of lesser GM cars, the division was able to shave $700 off the price of its base series, creating in the process a new breed of automobile in a heretofore untapped price class.

Here, then, was a Cadillac priced about $500 above cars of the Buick-Chrysler class—a big leap, to be sure, in the mid-thirties, but less than half the premium that the purchase of a Cadillac would have required only one year earlier. Not surprisingly, Cadillac sales

more than trebled.

It's easy to imagine the scene that must have taken place over on East Grand Boulevard, where Packards were being turned out in record numbers. Packard, of course, had brought forth in 1935 its One-Twenty (see SIA #47) priced to compete with the mid-range Buicks and straight-eight LaSalles (see SIA #40). It was proving to be a resounding success. But between the One-Twenty and the senior Packard Eight lay a price spread of some $1300. Or to put it another way, one could buy two of the smaller models for less than the price of the cheapest "big" Packard.

Cadillac's message was not lost upon President Alvan Macauley and the rest of the Packard management. By 1939 they, too, were mating the eight-cylinder engine of the larger Packard to the body (and to some extent the chassis) of the One-Twenty—thereby dropping the price of their Super Eight by more than a thousand dollars.

The year 1940 saw, along with the demise of the great Packard Twelve, the advent of a brand new engine for the senior cars, called by then the One-Sixty

and One-Eighty. A flathead, nine-main-bearing straight-eight like its predecessor, the silky-smooth new powerplant was of shorter-stroke design, larger displacement (356 versus 320 cubic inches), and greatly increased horsepower (160 @ 3500 rpm versus 130 @ 3200). And to make the deal even more attractive, another $100 was shaved off the price of the Super Eight-cum-One-Sixty, giving it a $90 price advantage compared with Cadillac's series Sixty-Two. A 43 percent increase in the production of Packard's One-Sixty was the result.

By 1941, however, Packard was due for a major restyling. A new, narrower grille had been fitted to the 1940 models. They were handsome automobiles indeed, and they sold well, but basically the bodies were those of the 1938 Packard. Three years was considered the maximum, in those days, for the production run of a given design, so something new was in order.

That "something new" was not, in the eyes of many observers, new enough. The 1941 Packard's sheet metal had been redesigned, all right, but its styling

motif was straight out of the mid-thirties. So, while the design has stood rather well the test of time, at its introduction it looked hopelessly dated. Nor was Packard's 8½ percent price boost any boon to sales.

Perhaps Packard realized its error even before the 1941 models were introduced in October 1940. For, just five months later the Clipper, a dramatic new Packard powered by a tuned-up version of the One-Twenty engine, made its debut (see *SIA #59*). The Clipper promptly became the company's best-selling line, and when the 1942 models arrived, Clipper styling had been extended both up and down the scale, encompassing the senior Packards as well as the lower-priced six.

Not that styling problems were the sole source of Packard's eroding position in the new, upper-medium price bracket. Competition from Cadillac was becoming increasingly fierce.

Nineteen-forty had marked the last year for the LaSalle, Cadillac's handsome, bargain-priced junior edition. Its final season had been a moderately successful one, though production was only about three-fourths of the marque's 1937 peak. But evidently the Cadillac management figured—correctly, as matters developed—that what the car needed was the Cadillac nameplate. Accordingly, both the LaSalle and the Cadillac Sixty-Two were replaced for the 1941 season by two new Cadillacs, a brand new Sixty-One and a revised Sixty-Two, the latter priced $250 lower than its 1940 counterpart.

The Sixty-One, less expensive by $50 than the Sixty-Two, was Cadillac's best seller that year. It used GM's dashing new fastback "B" body, while the Sixty-Two wore a beautifully updated version

*Top and above center: Cadillac's hood trim is more decorative than functional, while Packard's also holds its hood release levers. **Above and above right:** 1941 was the first year Cadillac hid its gas filler in the taillamp housing. Packard settled for keeping it behind a door. **Right and far right:** Cadillac used functional rubber splash shield on rear fenders. Packard preferred flashier stainless trim.*

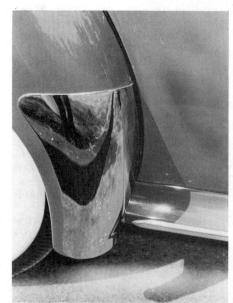

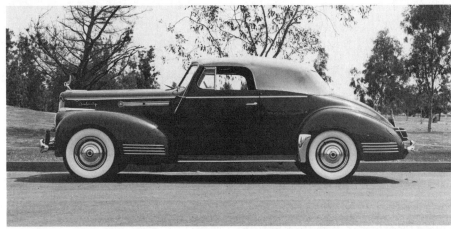

Left and below: Some Cadillac enthusiasts consider the 1941 convertible one of the best looking Cadillacs ever. Packard combines dashing good looks with traditional styling themes. Bottom left and bottom: Cadillac sidelamps are integrated into egg-crate grille design. Packard mounted theirs in separate pods atop headlamps and fenders.

of 1940's "C" shell. Wheelbase for both series stood at 126 inches, splitting the difference between the Cadillac and LaSalle of the year before. The engine was that of the 1940 Cadillac, given an extra 15 horsepower, chiefly by means of redesigned, high-compression cylinder heads. And prices commenced at only $125 above that of the cheapest LaSalle of the year before. Thus a Cadillac, a genuine Cadillac (for all of its resemblance to lesser GM marques) could be had for as little as $1345 f.o.b. Detroit—just $104 more than the Buick Century, and $400 less than the rival Packard One-Sixty.

No wonder Packard was hurting! Production of the two smaller Cadillacs was up nearly 80 percent over the combined total of 1940's LaSalle and Cadillac Sixty-Two. Sales of the Packard One-Sixty, meanwhile, slipped by more than a third.

Comparative sales figures aside, what had taken place over the half-decade that culminated in the handsome new 1941 models was the creation of an entirely new class of automobile. Cars had improved so much over the preceding 15 years—in performance, comfort, durability and looks—that apart from their ostentation (which, during hard times, the well-to-do had generally found it prudent to avoid) the all-out luxury models had little to offer that justified their premium price. (The eight-cylinder Cadillac Sixty of 1937, for instance, would readily outperform the company's V-12—and with no loss of smoothness—though it sold for less than half the price of the larger car.)

And so, in these new Cadillacs and Packards the middle-class motorist found a new standard of quality and performance at a price he could afford.

Luxury features abounded. Cadillac offered its first automatic transmission, the Hydra-matic, as an option in its 1941 models; Packard countered with the Electro-Matic clutch. Both Cad and Packard, and Lincoln as well, supplied hydraulic valve lifters in the interest of quieter operation. Packard had introduced refrigerated air conditioning

the year before, a "first" for the industry, and Cadillac now followed suit. Both were heavy, cumbersome, expensive units, not notably satisfactory in their operation. But they nevertheless represented a major breakthrough in passenger comfort, and they set the pattern for times yet to come.

It was *SIA*'s good fortune to locate, within a reasonable distance of each other, particularly choice examples of both the Cadillac Sixty-Two and the Packard One-Sixty. And we brought them together for our comparison-testing and Jim Tanji's photo session at a point midway between the homes of their respective owners.

The two cars make an interesting comparison, and in some respects a marked contrast. In weight, wheelbase and overall length they are very much alike, but the Cadillac is three inches lower and eight inches wider than the Packard, giving it—depending upon one's perspective—either a "more modern" or a "less classic" appearance than its rival.

The Packard has the edge when it comes to horsepower, but both cars are so strong that the difference is scarcely noticeable. More significant is the easy down-the-road gait of the Packard when the overdrive is engaged. Nothing wrong with the Cadillac's highway manners

*Right and far right: Packard's wheelcovers contain myriad concentric rings; Cadillac's are almost severely plain. **Below far right:** Cadillac's rear fender skirts were standard equipment. **Below and below center:** Both cars use quite similar chromed rear fender accents. **Bottom left and right:** Packard's hood has more traditional right and left side openings, while Cadillac uses one-piece "alligator" style opening for access to its innards.*

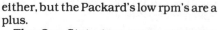

comparisonReport

either, but the Packard's low rpm's are a plus.

The One-Sixty is a more expensive automobile than its competitor from GM, of course, and the difference shows up in a number of interesting ways—some of them scarcely apparent to the casual observer. The Packard's nine-main-bearing straight eight, for instance, is even silkier than the Cadillac's three-bearing V-8. Roller bearings—costlier than the more commonly used ball bearings—are employed almost exclusively in the senior Packards of this era, and the sophisticated Packard front suspension is virtually identical to that of the postwar Rolls-Royce.

Other features, less significant from an engineering standpoint, are more likely to meet the eye. There are the impressive, triple-trumpet horns, for example, the chromed stone shields on the rear fenders, the hidden trunk hinges, and of course the gorgeous pelican mascot perched above the radiator grille.

Our comparisonReport Packard happens to be a deluxe model, which means among other things that the window sills are crafted of fine inlaid hardwoods, and the upholstery is Bedford cord trimmed with pig-grained cowhide, instead of the metal window frames and the plain leather interior featured on the standard convertibles. This particular car, by the way, bears body # 1—the first deluxe convertible produced for 1941 in the One-Sixty series.

The Cadillac, with its eight inches of additional width, is by a substantial

Left and below: Packard dash is a riot of rectangles right down to the shape of the control knobs. Cadillac goes both rectangular and round.

margin the roomier of the two cars. This is particularly evident in the back seat, both in terms of width and knee room. Neither car could be considered spacious in the rear quarters, but the Packard is downright cramped.

In both cars, front seat legroom is more than adequate even for a tall driver, and entry and egress are easy. Given its lower overall height we were surprised to note that the Cadillac's front cushion is noticeably higher than that of the Packard, a decided plus. The Packard, however, provides marginally better support to the lower back.

Visibility to the side is poor in the Cadillac, worse in the Packard. In 1941, Detroit—Chrysler excepted—had not yet fitted rear quarter windows to their convertible coupes. The blind spot can be a problem in parking the car, and downright hazardous when entering a busy intersection.

Nor is vision to the rear any better. Both cars came equipped with minuscule backlights, typical of convertibles at that time. Our comparisonReport Cadillac, however, has been retrofitted with a large transparent panel to the rear—a big help. We wonder why Detroit hadn't tumbled to that idea by 1941.

Dash layouts are similar to the extent that both cars carry a full array of gauges and are equipped with dashboard clocks as well. The Cadillac's layout is splashier, featuring liberal use of chrome along with huge, circular dials for the speedometer and chronometer, the former being flanked by the customary monitors. Instruments on the Packard's dash, on the other hand, are smaller, giving the car's interior a smart, understated look.

Both cars fire up promptly and take off with cushy smoothness. The Cadillac's clutch action is downright creamy, and it's easy to see why this transmission was such a favorite among hotrodders of a generation ago. Shifts are a breeze! The Packard is no slouch in that department, either, but we found that unless care is exercised it's easy to override the synchronizers and clash the

1941 Table of Prices*

	Cadillac Sixty-One	Cadillac Sixty-Two	Packard One-Sixty
Coupe, 2-passenger	—	—	$1594
Coupe, 2-4 passenger	—	$1420	$1709
Coupe, 2-4 pass., deluxe	$1345	—	—
Coupe, 5-passenger	$1345	—	—
Coupe, 5-pass., deluxe	$1435	—	—
Sedan, 5-passenger	$1445	$1495	$1750
Sedan, 5-pass., deluxe	$1535	$1585	—
Convertible coupe	—	—	$1892
Conv. coupe, deluxe	—	$1645	$2067
Convertible sedan	—	—	$2180
Conv. sedan, deluxe	—	$1965	$2405
Sedan, 5-pass., 138" w/b	—	—	$2009
Sedan, 7-pass., 148" w/b	—	—	$2161
Limousine, 148" w/b	—	—	$2289

Note: The above table is misleading to the extent that the trim levels of the Packard sedans and 2-4 passenger coupes were at least the equivalent of the "deluxe" Cadillacs. Similarly, equipment was not comparable in some instances. Accordingly, prices should be compared with caution.

Sources: *Automotive Industries*, October 15, 1940; Robert E. Turnquist, *The Packard Story*

*Prices at time of introduction

Comparison Chart: 1941 Luxury Convertibles

	Cadillac Sixty-Two	Packard One-Sixty
Price, f.o.b. factory	$1645	$1892
Engine (type)	L-head V-8	L-Head straight 8
Bore x stroke (inches)	3.5 x 4.5	3.5 x 4.625
Displacement	346.0 cubic inches	356.0 cubic inches
Compression ratio	7.25:1	6.45:1
Bhp @ rpm	150 @ 3400	160 @ 3600
Torque @ rpm	283 @ 1700	292 @ 1800
Carburetor	Dual downdraft	Dual downdraft
Electrical system	6-volt, Delco-Remy	6-volt, Auto-Lite
Clutch (type)	Single dry plate	Single dry plate
Diameter	10.5 inches	11 inches
Standard transmission	3-speed manual	3-speed manual
Ratios (:1)	2.39/1.53/1.00	2.43/1.53/1.00
Differential (type)	Hypoid	Hypoid
Drive axles	Semi-floating	Semi-floating
Ratio	3.77:1	3.92:1
Steering (type)	Worm & nut	Worm & roller
Ratio (gear)	23.6:1	20.3:1
Turns, lock-to-lock	5.125	4.75
Turning radius	22'9"	22'6"
Brakes (type)	Hydraulic, drum	Hydraulic, drum
Drum diameter	12 inches	12 inches
Effective area	208.0 square inches	196.0 inches
Front suspension	Independent coil springs	Independent coil springs
Front tread	59 inches	59 3/16 inches
Rear tread	63 inches	59 15/16 inches
Capacities		
Crankcase	7 quarts	7 quarts
Cooling system	25 quarts	20 quarts
Fuel tank	20 gallons	20 gallons
Shipping weight	4055 pounds	3965 pounds*
Measurements		
Wheelbase	126 inches	127 inches
Overall length	216 inches	206.1875 inches
Overall width	80 inches	72 inches
Overall height	64.5 inches	67.5 inches
Minimum road clearance	8 inches	8.5 inches
Tire size	7.00 x 15	7.00 x 16
Production/Registrations		
Registrations (all series)	60,242	69,653
Production (model year, all series)	66,130	72,855
Production (model year, this series)	24,726	3,525
Performance factors		
Hp/c.i.d.	.43	.45
Lbs/hp	27.03	24.78
Lbs/c.i.d.	11.72	11.14
Performance**		
Top speed	95.2 mph	95.0 mph
Fuel mileage	15.3 mpg	16.2 mpg

*Base convertible coupe
**General Motors Proving Grounds test, 5/12/41

gears. We suspect that this may have more to do with the condition of the transmission in this particular car than with the design of the unit, however.

Huge steering wheels, a foot-and-a-half in diameter, make easy work of turning both cars. The Packard's steering is a little quicker, a trifle easier, a tad more precise, but both are excellent in this respect—particularly for cars of this vintage.

The Cad seems to be a little better insulated against road noise, and its ride is definitely softer and smoother than that of the Packard—important features in a luxury car. Still, this may be a mixed blessing since the One-Sixty's handling edge presumably stems from its relatively firm suspension.

Brakes on both cars are calculated to inspire confidence on the part of the driver. They're really very, very good. Here again we'd have to give a slight edge to the Packard, because less pedal pressure is required to bring the car to a halt.

The acceleration of these big, heavy automobiles isn't going to send anyone to the chiropractor with a dislocated neck, but it's brisk enough to make both cars a joy to drive. We'd judge them about equal in that respect. And both are capable of idling down to 10 miles an hour or less, then moving out in top gear with turbine-like smoothness.

Victor and Jennette Fink's Cadillac is part of an eclectic collection of seven cars, including two other Cadillacs, a V-12 Packard and assorted other collector vehicles. It came to the Finks in 1980 from the estate of the late Owen Owens, fully restored by its previous owner. Back in 1941 it had been a special-order job featuring an unusual Bedford cord interior and non-stock brown metallic paint. Its present mileage of 76,000 is believed to be original. The Cad could easily be made into a show car, but Vic and Jennette prefer to maintain it as a "driver." Seen regularly on Cadillac-LaSalle club tours, the car has taken its owners—comfortably and dependably—on trips of up to 400 miles.

Clarence and Elizabeth Blixt's Pack-

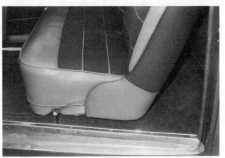

*Facing page: Cadillac door panels are rather plain; Packard uses woodgrain and fabric along with leather. **This page, left:** Two silky, superb powerplants: Cadillac's bulletproof flathead V-8 and Packard's silent straight eight. **Below left and below:** Both cars offer posh seating. **Below left center:** driveReport Cadillac has unusual fabric seats instead of leather. **Below center and bottom:** Performance? Take your pick. The cars are so evenly matched it really comes down to personal preference in such areas as engine configuration and styling.*

ard, on the other hand, was a discouraging sight when first they beheld it, back in 1974. It was no better when they bought it four years later from Clarence's brother, and a full, frame-up restoration was undertaken. Clarence handled the mechanical end himself, farming out the body work, paint and upholstery to specialists.

The Blixt car, too, is part of a collection, though Clarence—co-founder with his brother of the Northern California chapter of Packards International—is more of a specialist than Victor Fink. Apart from a 1958 Mercedes Benz 190SL which Elizabeth drives, the Blixt stable is filled with five Packards, including our comparisonReport car.

The question is inevitable, of course: Which would we choose, if it were 1941 all over again and we were prosperous enough to be shopping for a car of this caliber? It's no easy choice!

• There's a 20 percent price differential between the two cars. Score one for Cadillac; for sheer dollar value it's hard to beat.

• On the other hand, we spend a fair amount of time in the Sierras, and the quicker steering and more precise handling of the Packard would be an important plus.

• But again, sometimes we carry a car full of people, and the Cadillac is by far the roomier of the two convertibles.

• But wait! We also like to cruise the open highways of the Golden State, and the Packard's overdrive is a highly desirable feature for that purpose.

• Then again, slam a door on the Cadillac, and you begin to see what the "Body by Fisher" slogan was all about. Solid! There's nothing flimsy about the Packard's structure, but here the advantage is plainly Cadillac's.

• Styling? A subjective judgment, obviously. The '41 Cadillac's architecture was a harbinger of postwar styling trends (and a whole lot better looking, in our view, than anything Cadillac built for the ensuing several years). That year's Packard, on the other hand, was the last of the classically styled cars from that master builder. To the uninitiated it could easily pass for a mid-thirties automobile. Whether that is good or bad depends, of course, on one's perspective.

Unfortunately, the Packard One-Sixty

also looks very much like the company's junior cars. It's 400 pounds heavier than the One-Twenty, with half the additional weight accounted for by that superb, big engine and the rest distributed among various other components. But the wheelbase, the body shell and the general styling themes of the two cars are the same. That similarity was no help to sales of the senior series.

Cadillac, of course, had no such problem.

Taken all-in-all we'd have to call it a standoff between the Packard and the Cad. And to tell the truth, if it were 1941 again, with World War II raging ever closer, we'd be disinclined to buy either one of these fine cars. Both Victor Fink and Clarence Blixt report fuel mileage in the 12 to 13 mile-per-gallon range—not enough, at a time when gas rationing was obviously soon to come. "For the duration," to use the popular phrase of that day, we'd have preferred a car with a daintier appetite!

But as for today, we'd gladly settle for one of each! □

About the setting: Our photo session for this comparisonReport was held at the Livermore (California) Municipal Airport. In the background of some of Jim Tanji's photographs there appears a Royal Canadian Air Force plane of 1941 vintage, a Harvard Mark II. Updated to Mark IV specifications in 1952, it now belongs to John Bassett, of Fremont, California.

Acknowledgements and Bibliography
Automotive Industries (various issues); James D. Bell, "The Cadillac Standard," Automobile Quarterly, Volume 3, Number 3; Chilton's Auto Repair Manual, 1940-1953; Jerry Heasley, The Production Figure Book for US Cars; Maurice D. Hendry, Cadillac: The Complete History; Richard M. Langworth, Encyclopedia of American Cars, 1940-1970; Ralph Stein, The American Automobile; Robert E. Turnquist, The Packard Story. Our thanks to John Bassett, Fremont, California; Ralph Dunwoodie, Sun Valley, Nevada; Don Figone, San Bruno, California; Russell N. Head, Hillsborough, California. Special thanks to Clarence and Elizabeth Blixt, Escalon, California; Victor and Jennette Fink, Burlingame, California.

1948 Cadillac 61
The First Shall Be Last

by Arch Brown
photos by Bud Juneau

IT isn't very often that one encounters a totally original, 50-year-old automobile that is still in really presentable condition. We found this one, of all places, at a Vintage Chevrolet Club meet. It's a 1948 Cadillac Sixty-One coupe, popularly known as a "sedanet." This model, as Cadillac aficionados are aware, represented the least expensive car in the entire Cadillac line, with a base price of just $2,728. But of course the "bottom of the line" at Cadillac still represents a distinctly upscale automobile. And its original price tag, though a bargain by just about anyone's standards, was $431 (19 percent) higher than the corresponding Buick Roadmaster—which of course was a luxurious machine in its own right.

One might think of the 1948 line as both the Alpha and the Omega at Cadillac. All but the out-sized Fleetwood Seventy-Five models bore a completely redesigned body that year, representing GM's first really new postwar styling effort. Thus the "Alpha" designation. And on the other hand, the monobloc, flathead V-8, which dated from 1936, represented the "Omega," for it was making its final appearance for '48. When 1949 rolled around there would be a brand new V-8, featuring oversquare design, high compression and overhead valves.

Which, by the bye, takes nothing away from the venerable Cadillac flathead, which, in combination with the Hydra-Matic transmission, had given an excellent account of itself during wartime, powering first the M-5 light tanks (two engines, two transmissions per unit), and by 1944 the M-24 light tank. Cadillac's durability and reliability were put to the most rigorous of tests during the war, and they passed with flying colors.

At 364.6 cubic inches, the 1948 engine is slightly larger than the forthcoming 1949 mill, though it doesn't have quite the performance potential of its successor. But on the other hand, it has been our experience that the flathead is both smoother and quieter than 1949's overhead valve job. And if its 150 horsepower is ten short of that of the later

Originally published in Special Interest Autos #171, May-June 1999 engine, we found it to be more than adequate for the job of propelling this two-ton-plus automobile. We don't run any races with our driveReport subjects, obviously, but General Motors proving grounds records show this model with a top speed of 93.3 miles per hour; and according to the same source, the run from rest to 60 mph is made in 16.3 seconds. By 1948 standards, these are rather impressive figures, and Cadillac's claim of lively acceleration was certainly borne out during our test drive.

This, by the way, despite the fact that the engine in our driveReport car is obviously tired. The odometer registers something over 22,000 miles, doubtless on its second trip around the clock, and as best we have been able to determine, the heads have never been off. Owner Doug Dauterman tells us that when he first acquired the car "it smoked like Humphrey Bogart," though no such problem was encountered during our test drive.

We started and stopped the engine several times in the course of Bud Juneau's photo session, and it never failed to fire at the first turn. Steering seems a little heavy, now that we're all accustomed to the ease of a power assist; yet the wheel turns more easily than that of a good many cars of the immediate postwar era. Nor is it excessively slow: Just four turns of the big wheel are required to take it from lock-to-lock, giving the Cad remarkably good maneuverability for a car of this size and weight.

The transmission surges, as the early HydraMatics always do, as it changes from gear to gear. This is particularly noticeable in the shift from First to Second, which represents a jump in ratio from 3.97 to 2.55. But if the driver's foot doesn't lay too heavily upon the accelerator, the action of the transmission is comparatively smooth thereafter. Once in fourth gear, the Cadillac glides along in near-silence; and then when the accelerator is punched, the HydraMatic down-shifts to third speed for quicker acceleration. We found the Cad to be an exhilarating car to drive, despite its considerable heft.

These old Cadillacs provide a marvelously smooth ride, but the shocks in this particular car are clearly worn out, which makes it impossible for us to give a fair evaluation of the Cad's potential in that respect. In the turns, the car leans more heavily than one might wish; and there's a floating situation when a dip is encountered. But despite the handicap posed by the poor shocks, we experienced no loss of control in our limited test drive.

The brakes are powerful, as befits a heavy car. Owner Doug Dauterman recently had them completely overhauled, but they still have a mild but discon-

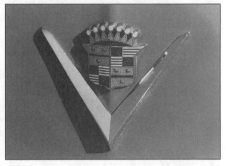

Top: All-new front end styling still carried traditional Cadillac appearance. ***Above left:*** "Sombrero" wheel covers were carried over from earlier cars. ***Right:*** It wouldn't be a Cadillac without the V and traditional crest. ***Below left and right:*** Tailfins were a styling sensation when introduced and began a Cadillac tradition. Flip-up taillamps were another Caddy trademark. ***Bottom:*** Sleekest of the '48 line was also the cheapest at $2,728. f.o.b.

Above: Caddy script accents front fenders. **Below left:** *Flip-up taillamp/gas filler actually originated on earlier cars and was a carryover for '48.* **Right:** *All-new styling gave a modern yet conservative look except for the fins.* **Bottom:** *Another assurance of quality.* **Facing page:** *Handling is typical of big, heavy US cars of the time.*

certing tendency to pull to the left. To date, Doug has been unable to determine the cause.

The parking brake is more effective than most, but it is nevertheless prudent to "lock" the transmission when the car is parked. The technique here is to kill the engine while the transmission quadrant is in the "Lo" position, then move the lever to Reverse, which immobilizes the Cadillac. The transmission quadrant is typical of all the early General Motors automatics: N - D - L - R. This layout was useful for rocking the car out of mud or snow, but over the years it occasionally led to difficulties, and in a few cases, reportedly, to tragedy. The problem was that drivers accustomed to the three-speed manual shift (as nearly all of us were, in 1948) tended to pull down on the transmission control lever, expecting to engage Low gear, only to find that the transmission had been shifted into Reverse. Eventually, of course, the quadrant was standardized, just as the three-speed floorshift pattern had been standardized in 1928.

Leg room is ample in front, and knee room is adequate to the rear, despite the fastback design. This represents a trade-off, however, for in order to provide an acceptable level of space, the rear seat backrest is positioned nearly vertically. This, we think, could be an invitation to big-time discomfort on a long trip. Rearward visibility has never been a strong point with fastback cars, but the window in this car is big enough to give the driver a fairly good over-the-

1948 Cadillac Prices, Weights and Production

	Price	Weight	Production
Series Sixty-One, 126-inch wheelbase			
Sedanet (club coupe), 5 passenger	$2,728	4,068	3,521
Sedan, 4-door, 5-passenger	2,833	4,150	5,081
Chassis only	n/a	N/A	1
TOTAL PRODUCTION, SERIES SIXTY-ONE			8,603
Series Sixty-Two, 126-inch wheelbase			
Sedanet (club coupe), 5-passenger	2,912	4,125	4,764
Sedan, 4-door, 5-passenger	2,996	4,179	23,997
Convertible coupe, 5-passenger	3,442	4,449	5,450
Chassis only	N/A	N/A	2
TOTAL PRODUCTION, SERIES SIXTY-TWO			34,213
Series Fleetwood Sixty-Special, 133-inch wheelbase			
Sedan, 4-door, 5-passenger	3,820	4,356	6,561
Series Fleetwood Seventy-Five, 136-inch wheelbase			
Sedan, 5-passenger	4,779	4,875	225
Sedan, 7-passenger	4,999	4,878	499
Business sedan, 9-passenger	4,679	4,780	90
Imperial sedan, 7-passenger	5,199	4,959	382
Business Imperial, 9-passenger	4,868	4,839	64
Chassis only (163-inch wheelbase)	N/A	N/A	2
TOTAL PRODUCTION, SERIES FLEETWOOD 75			1,261
GRAND TOTAL, 1948 MODEL YEAR PRODUCTION:			50,638
TOTAL 1948 CALENDAR YEAR PRODUCTION:			66,209

shoulder view from the inside mirror.

Seat cushions are soft, almost like living room sofas. Personally, we'd prefer something a little firmer, but perhaps this is part of the Cad's luxury image. The upholstery must have been covered throughout most of the Cadillac's life, for it appears almost new. Similarly, the woodgraining on the window sills is in excellent condition. Doug Dauterman has been told that the original owner would not permit his passengers to rest their elbows on the window sills. Neither would he permit smoking in the car. The woodgraining on the dash could use a bit of attention, presumably as the result of sunburn, but otherwise the interior is in amazingly good shape.

The instrument panel is one of the most attractive ever devised. In Dick Langworth's words, it is "dominated by a huge, ornate drum-type housing for the speedometer, minor gauges and controls." Langworth goes on to explain, with obvious regret, that "this lasted only a year, because it was complicated and costly to produce."

The Cadillac's exterior finish looks better than anyone would have a right to expect, after 50 years. The paint is worn thin on the crown of the right front fender, and a faded spot on the right door

1948 Luxury Club Coupes Compared

	Cadillac 61	Lincoln	Packard Super 8
Base price	$2,728	$2,533	$2,665
Wheelbase	126″	125″	120″
Overall length	214″	218.0625″	204.625″
Overall width	79″	77.83″	77.47″
Overall height	67.5″	67.125″	64.0625″
Front track	59″	59″	59.594″
Rear track	63″	60.6875″	60.72″
Weight (lb.)	4,068	3,915	3,790
Engine	V-8	V-12	Straight-8
Displacement (cu. in.)	346.4	292.0	327.1
Compression ratio	7.25:1	7.20:1	7.00:1
Horsepower @ rpm	150/3,400	125/3,600	145/3,600
Torque @ rpm	253/1,600	214/1,600	266/2,000
Valve configuration	L-head	L-head	L-head
Carburetor	Dual downdraft	Dual downdraft	Dual downdraft
Clutch	Dry plate	Dry plate	Dry plate
Outside diameter	10.5″	10″	10.5″
Standard transmission	3-speed	3-speed	3-speed
Optional transmission	HydraMatic	Overdrive	Overdrive
Final drive ratio (standard)	3.77:1	4.22:1*	3.90:1**
Steering	Recirc. ball	Worm/roller	Worm/roller
Ratio	21.3:1	22.5:1	26.2:1
Braking area (sq. in.)	208.0	184.0	171.5
Drum diameter	12″	12″	12″
Tire size	8.20/15	7.00/15	7.00/15
Stroke/bore ratio	1.286:1	1.304:1	1.214:1
Crankshaft revs per mile	2,650	3,038	2,808
Horsepower per c.i.d.	.433	.428	.443
Weight (lb.) per h.	27.1	31.3	26.1
Weight per c.i.d.	11.7	13.4	11.6

Above: 1948 marked the last year of the venerable 348 flathead, which had proven itself in peace and war. *Above right:* Original sales agreement for driveReport car. *Below left:* Great-looking instrument cluster design was used only in '48. *Right:* Bin-style glove compartment is placed logically in middle of dash. *Facing Page:* Fastback sacrifices trunk space for style. Original tools are still in their factory-supplied bag.

1948 Cadillac 61

gives evidence of a minor repair somewhere along the way. Otherwise, the finish is almost as good as it appears here in Bud's photographs.

We were moderately surprised to find that this is not a heavily optioned automobile. In so many cases, during the early postwar years, dealers — who literally had customers standing in line, awaiting the opportunity to purchase a new car — tended to load each new automobile with options in order to increase their profit margin. The list of extras on this car is short, but well chosen: HydraMatic transmission, radio with antenna, "sombrero" wheel covers, white sidewall tires, day/night (flip-type) mirror, left outside mirror, and — oddly enough — a single backup light. Most of us are accustomed to thinking of backup lights in pairs, but they didn't necessarily come that way in 1948.

It's all a matter of personal preference, of course, but the 1948 Cadillac "eggcrate" grille, taller and narrower than the 1949 edition and bolder than the '41, has always had a special appeal for

this writer. But the styling feature that provoked the most comment when these cars were introduced was the little fins that rode atop the rear fenders. The inspiration for these fins, which became the industry's major fad during the 1950s, can be traced back to 1940, when GM styling director Harley Earl sent several members of his staff to Selfridge Field, near Detroit, for a look at the new Lockheed P-38 Lightning fighter plane, the twin-tailed hotshot that the Germans dubbed "Der Gabelschwanzteufel," or "Two-Tailed Devil." So intrigued was this group of stylists that, according to Walter M. P. McCall, they "went back to their drawing boards and translated some of the Lightning's radical features into styling concepts for possible cars of the future." This accounts not only for the fins, but also for the simulated air scoops on the leading edge of the rear fenders of our featured Cadillac.

(Truthfully, as Bill Mitchell, head stylist at Cadillac when our driveReport car was developed, once commented to journalist Dick Langworth, the original fin was "merely a humped-up taillight, really, it wasn't a fin at all." But the fins, or whatever they were, provided Cadillac

with as clear an identity from the rear as it had when viewed from the front. Langworth quotes GM Chairman Alfred Sloan as saying to Cadillac General Manager Jack Gordon, "Jack, now you have a Cadillac in the rear as well as in the front.")

So our driveReport Cadillac was a trail-blazer in terms of styling.

And, by the bye, the left-side fin is hinged, revealing a small, illuminated compartment in which the gasoline filler cap is hidden. A clever touch, and a convenient one.

There's an interesting sidelight concerning the body shell used by the 1948 Series Sixty-One, Sixty-Two and Fleetwood Sixty-Special Cadillacs, as well as the Oldsmobile Ninety-Eight. Known officially as the GM "C" body, it had originally been intended as the corporate "B" body. In a 1993 letter to this writer, the late Richard H. Stout, a General Motors stylist when these cars were built, explained, "This is why wheelbases on the new jobs were the same as the old B-body and three inches shorter than the previous ones. GM simply did not have time to get a C-body done, so this was rechristened C from B. Cadillac had to be first with some all new stuff." (During 1942-47 the Sixty-One had employed the then current B-body on a 126-inch wheelbase, while the Sixty-Two used the larger C-body on a 129-inch chassis. For 1948, both models employed the 126-inch wheelbase, fitted with the new B-cum-C body. A stretched version was employed for the Fleetwood Sixty-Special.)

Thanks to delays caused apparently by re-tooling for the new body, the 1948 Cadillacs weren't introduced until March of that year. Long before that, prospective buyers had been standing in line, awaiting their chance to buy a new Cadillac; and of course the new model

illustrations by Russell von Sauers, The Graphic Automobile Studio

specifications

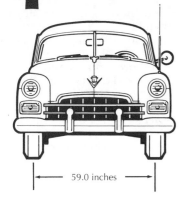

← 59.0 inches →

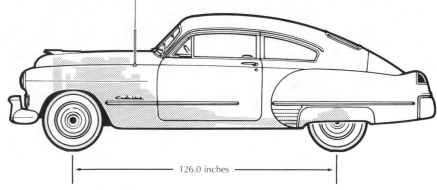

← 126.0 inches →

1948 Cadillac 61

Price	$2,728 f.o.b. factory, with standard equipment
Options on dR car	HydraMatic transmission, radio with antenna, white sidewall tires, left outside mirror, day/night mirror, backup light

ENGINE

Type	90-degree L-head V-8
Bore x stroke	3.5 inches x 4.5 inches
Displacement	346.4 cubic inches
Compression ratio	7.25:1
Horsepower @ rpm	150 @ 3,400 (gross)
Torque @ rpm	283 @ 1,600 (gross)
Taxable horsepower	39.2
Valve configuration	L-head
Valve lifters	Hydraulic
Main bearings	3
Fuel system	1.25-inch dual downdraft carburetor, camshaft pump
Lubrication system	Pressure
Cooling system	Centrifugal pump
Exhaust system	Single
Electrical system	6-volt battery/coil

TRANSMISSION

Type	HydraMatic 4-speed automatic planetary
Ratios: 1st	3.97:1
2nd	2.55:1
3rd	1.55:1
4th	1.00:1
Reverse	3.74:1

DIFFERENTIAL

Type	Hypoid
Ratio	3.36:1
Drive axles	Semi-floating

STEERING

Type	Saginaw recirculating ball
Turns lock-to-lock	4
Ratio	25.6:1 gear
Turning diameter	45 feet 7 inches

BRAKES

Type	4-wheel internal hydraulic
Drum diameter	12 inches
Effective area	208 square inches

CHASSIS & BODY

Construction	Body-on-frame
Frame	Channel section steel with central X-member
Body construction	All steel
Body type	Sedanet (fastback club coupe)

SUSPENSION

Front	Independent A-arms, coil springs, torsional stabilizer bar
Rear	Rigid axle, semi-elliptic longitudinal springs
Shock absorbers	Lever hydraulic
Tires	8.20/15 4-ply
Wheels	Pressed steel, drop-center rims

WEIGHTS AND MEASURES

Wheelbase	126 inches
Overall length	214 inches
Overall width	79 inches
Overall height	66.75 inches
Front track	59 inches
Rear track	63 inches
Min. road clearance	8 inches
Shipping weight	4,068 pounds

CAPACITIES

Crankcase	7 quarts
Cooling system	26 quarts
Fuel tank	20 gallons

CALCULATED DATA

Horsepower per c.i.d.	.433
Weight per hp	27.1 pounds
Weight per c.i.d.	11.7 pounds
P.S.I. (brakes)	19.6
Stroke/bore ratio	1.286:1
Crankshaft rev/mile	2,650

PERFORMANCE

Top speed	93.3 mph
0-60 mph	16.3 seconds

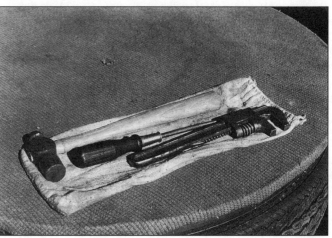

1948 Cadillac 61

brought an increase in demand. By year's end, Cadillac's total production totaled 66,209 cars. The total for the somewhat abbreviated model year came to 50,638 units.

It's interesting to note that while Cadillac's 1948 calendar year production represented an eleven percent increase over 1941, previously the division's all-time record. Meanwhile, output at all the other GM divisions actually fell. Specifically, Pontiac's volume was down by ten percent, Buick's by 13 percent, Oldsmobile's by 16 percent and Chevrolet's by 17 percent. It would be

1948

If 1998 was a less-than-felicitous time for Republicans, consider how they must have felt 50 years earlier, during the year when our driveReport Cadillac was built.

To refresh the reader's memory, that was the year when President Harry S. Truman pulled one of the great political upsets of all time by beating New York Governor Thomas E. Dewey in the race for the United States Presidency. Dewey's election had seemed assured, partly because Truman, who had inherited the presidency upon Franklin Roosevelt's death, had never been particularly popular; and partly because there were two "third party" candidates in the running, both of them representing spin-offs from the Democratic party. Former Vice President Henry A. Wallace was running to Harry Truman's left on the Progressive ticket, while South Carolina Governor J. Strom Thurmond rivaled Truman on the right as the candidate of the States Rights or "Dixiecrat" party. (And yes, this is the same Strom Thurmond who, at age 96, is still serving, at this writing, as the most senior member of the United States Senate.)

So certain of the results were the pundits, and nearly everyone else for that matter, that *Life* magazine had already gone to the printers with a photograph of "President Dewey" on the cover. But, in the end, Dewey captured only 16 states with 189 electoral votes against Truman's 28 states and 304 electoral votes.

And speaking of Franklin Roosevelt, on April 12th the third anniversary of his death was observed in London with the unveiling by his widow of a statue in Grosvenor Park. The entire Royal Family, as well as Winston Churchill, were on hand for the occasion.

Back in Washington, DC, Congress passed the Foreign Assistance Act, establishing the Economic Co-operation Administration, popularly known as the "Marshall Plan" after General George C. Marshall, President Truman's Secretary of State, who had originally proposed it. The purpose was to rehabilitate the economies of post World War II European nations in order to create

stable conditions in which free institutions could survive. Under the direction of former Studebaker president Paul G. Hoffman, $12 billion worth of economic aid was distributed over the next four years, in one of the most generous—and most successful—undertakings in the nation's history.

Of course, life had its brighter side. At the movies, Americans saw *Hamlet*, featuring Laurence Olivier; *Easter Parade*, starring Judy Garland; and *Treasure of the Sierra Madre*, with Humphrey Bogart and Walter Huston. And Jane Wyman, still married to Ronald Reagan in those days, won an Oscar for her role in *Johnny Belinda*, co-starring Lew Ayres.

And then, there were poignant moments, such as Babe Ruth's final public appearance, at the debut of the biographical motion picture *The Babe Ruth Story*. Three weeks later the Babe was dead, the victim of cancer. Still, all-in-all it was a happy time. The world was at peace, at least for the moment, and the economy was booming.

By way of illustrating how far recorded music has come in a comparatively short time, it was on June 21, 1948, that Dr. Peter Goldmark of the Columbia Broadcasting System demonstrated his "long-playing" (33 rpm) recordings. Until that time, phonograph turntables revolved at 78 rpm, limiting most of them to about a three-minute run. Of course, in the years that followed, Goldmark's triumph has been topped twice, first by tapes and more recently by CD's—with, we are told, more technological advances yet to come!

It wasn't a particularly outstanding year for popular music, perhaps because a number of the great songwriters, such as Jerome Kern and George Gershwin, were gone. Still, there were some good songs. Frank Loesser's "Once in Love with Amy," forever to be associated with Ray Bolger, and Cole Porter's "So In Love" come to mind, along with Sammy Cahn and Jule Styne's "It's Magic," a number made famous by Doris Day.

A three-cent stamp carried a first-class letter in those days; and the US Post Office

issued 29 distinct versions of it during 1948, honoring American historical events and noted Americans. Among those whose likeness appeared on these stamps were Elizabeth Cady Stanton, Carrie Chapman Catt and Lucretia Mott, pioneers in the cause of women's suffrage; Francis Scott Key, author of our national anthem; Clara Barton, founder of the American Red Cross; and the scientist Dr. George Washington Carver, the first African American ever to be so-honored.

Detroit, of course, was still enjoying the remnants of the post-war "seller's market." Ever since the end of World War II, demand for new cars had far exceeded the supply. And more than any other make, it was the Cadillac that was in demand. So much so, in fact, that dealers were confronted with the problem of customers who bought new Cadillacs at the government-imposed ceiling price, and then re-sold them on the "gray market" at an inflated figure.

Dealers fought back as best they could, often displaying considerable ingenuity in the process. Our driveReport Cadillac serves as case-in-point, for upon taking delivery of it, the original purchaser was required to sign an agreement stipulating that the car would not be sold or otherwise disposed of for a period of six months from the date of sale, without giving the dealer the option of re-purchasing the vehicle at the original purchase price, less sales tax and license fee. (A copy of this agreement appears on page 22.) Whether such a contract would stand up in court is debatable, of course; but this "Repurchase Option Agreement" serves to illustrate how seriously the dealers viewed the problem.

But still, new Cadillacs were rolling out of the factory in greater numbers than ever before in the division's history, and customers were literally standing in line, awaiting the opportunity to buy them. Nor was there any haggling over price. So when complaints were heard, they rarely came from Cadillac dealers.

The automobile industry had endured some very lean years. But by 1948, happy times had returned. Especially at Cadillac.

naive, however, to suggest that these figures accurately portrayed customer demand at that time. Critical materials, including sheet metal, were still in somewhat short supply during 1948; and there can be little doubt that General Motors executives, with an eye on the bottom line, were particularly generous in their allocations to the division that returned the highest per-unit profit.

(A similar pattern can be observed at Buick, by the way. There, the Roadmaster series represented 37.5 percent of the division's 1948 production, compared to just 4.2 percent during the 1941 model year.)

Cadillac fielded four distinct series of automobiles for 1948, down from six during the 1941 season. The '48s were late in arriving, having been introduced during March of that year, but surely they were worth the wait.

The entry-level Series Sixty-One was available in either of two body types, the coupe shown here and a four-door sedan.

Next up was the Sixty-Two, similar to the Sixty-One but featuring a somewhat higher level of equipment and trim, as well as a higher (by $184) price tag. It was offered in the same two body types, plus a smart convertible coupe.

For those who could afford it and had enough garage space to house it, there was the sumptuously trimmed and lavishly equipped Fleetwood Sixty-Special. Built on a 133-inch chassis and fitted with a stretched version of the new General Motors "C" body, it measured 225 21/32 inches bumper-to-bumper. Thus it was nearly a foot longer (as well as over $800 more costly) than the Sixty-Two.

And at the top, there was the Fleetwood "75" series, built on a 136-inch wheelbase and featuring styling that differed little from the 1941 version. These were Cadillac's most prestigious, as well as most expensive, cars, though they were only fractionally longer than the Sixty-Special. This series would have to wait until 1950 to be restyled, but so impressive were these warmed-over pre-war models that nobody really cared. Several variations were offered, ranging from a nine-passenger Business Sedan, intended primarily for the funeral trade, to a glamorous seven-passenger Imperial Sedan representing, at $5,199, the very acme of the Cadillac line.

We mentioned the HydraMatic transmission. Although it was an option, for which an extra $174 was charged, it was fitted to 97 percent of all new 1948 Cadillacs. (By 1952, the year after the Sixty-One was dropped from the line, the automatic would become standard issue for both the Sixty-Two and the Fleetwood Sixty-Special.)

Clubs and Specialists

Cadillac-LaSalle Club, Inc.
PO Box 1916
Lenoir, NC 28645-1916
828-757-9919; 828-757-0367 FAX
E-mail:cadlasal@twave.net
For Cadillac and LaSalle collectors and enthusiasts. 6,200 members with regions in 23 states.

Cadillac Drivers Club
5825 Vista Ave.
Sacramento, CA 95824
916-421-3193

Cadillac Past
14 Dudley Rd.
Billerica, MA 01821
508-667-0075

Ed Cholakian Enterprises, Inc.
12811 Foothill Blvd.
Sylmar, CA 91342
800-808-1147; 818-361-1147
818-361-9738 FAX
Specializing in Cadillac parts from 1940 to 1958.

F.E.N. Enterprises
PO Box 1559
Wappingers Falls, NY 12590
914-462-5959

Justin Hartley
17 Fox Meadow Lane
West Hartford, CT 06107-1216
860-523-0056; 860-604-9950 cellular
860-233-8840 FAX
Specializing in reprinted Cadillac shop manuals for all years through 1995.

Ted Holcombe Cadillac Parts
2933 Century Lane
Bensalem, PA 19020
215-245-4560

Honest John's Caddy Corner
PO Box 741-2271
Justin, TX 76247
940-648-3330

Kanter Auto Products
76 Monroe St.
Boonton, NJ 07005
800-526-1096

McVey's
5040 Antioch, Suite E
Merriam, KS 66203
913-722-0707

*Facing Page: Dashboard has a highly contemporary appearance. **This page, left:** High quality fit and materials throughout the interior. **Below left:** One of the very best aspects of the car. **Below:** AAA badge is another original touch on the Caddy.*

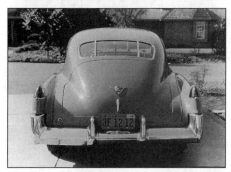

Best-equipped among the 1948 Cadillacs were the Fleetwood Seventy-Fives and the Sixty-Two convertibles, both lines being supplied with hydro-electric powered windows and seats. The latter feature was also furnished at no extra cost with the Sixty-Specials.

But for sheer value in a luxurious, high-quality, high-performance automobile, nothing, in 1948, could beat the $2,728 Cadillac Sixty-One sedanet. Don't you wish you could buy a new one just like it, at that price? ⌘

Acknowledgments and Bibliography

Automotive Industries, *March 15, 1948; Hendry, Maurice D.,* Cadillac: The Complete History *(Fourth edition); Kowalke, Ron (ed.),* Standard Catalog of American Cars, 1946-1975; *Langworth, Richard M.,* Encyclopedia of American Cars, 1940-1970; *Langworth, Richard M., "Of Tail Fins and V-8's,"* Automobile Quarterly, *Volume XIII, No. 3; Lamm, Michael, "Two Very Important Cars,"* Special Interest Autos *#11; McCall, Walter M.P.,* 80 Years of Cadillac-LaSalle.

Our thanks to Charles Carroll, Chico, California; Tom Dauterman, Chico, California; Bud Juneau, Brentwood, California. Special thanks to Doug Dauterman, Chico, California.

HOLLYWOODIE!

1949 CADILLAC SEVENTY-FIVE

by Arch Brown
photos by Bud Juneau

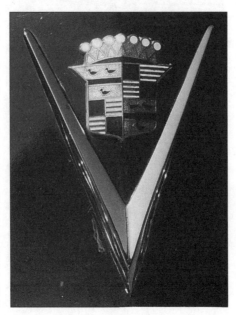

TO many collectors, the most desirable cars of the 1940s are the "woodies." And what an array of beauties that category encompasses! There's the pert little Ford Sportsman, the wooden-bodied convertible of 1946-48. There's Chrysler's magnificent Town and Country, supplied in both sedan and convertible form. And there's Buick's incomparable Estate Wagon.

But perhaps the most glamorous of all the woodies are those produced in minuscule numbers on long-wheelbase Cadillac chassis by Maurice Schwartz, of Pasadena, California. Schwartz, formerly a partner in the famed coachbuilding firm of Bohman and Schwartz, built a number of these stunning automobiles for such distinguished clients as cowboy star Gene Autry, shoe magnate Harry Karl (who purchased one as a gift for his wife, actress Marie McDonald), and Mexican president Miguel Aleman.

As Strother MacMinn tells the story in *SIA* #11, Maurice Schwartz was an old world craftsman, born in Austria. After serving his apprenticeship in his native country, he came to the United States in 1910. He was employed for several years by such distinguished firms as Fisher Brothers and Willoughby Coachbuilders, then came to California in 1918 to take a job with the Earl Carriage Works in Los Angeles.

In 1924 Schwartz joined Pasadena's Walter M. Murphy, Coachbuilders, working there until the organization folded in 1932. He then joined with Christian Bowman, another Murphy "alumnus," to form Bohman and Schwartz. That partnership was amicably dissolved in 1947, after which Maurice Schwartz — 63 years of age by that time — established his own firm. A few years later, though past 70, he began to take on restoration work for Bill Harrah, continuing in that endeavor until his death in 1961.

Between 1947 and 1949, six Cadillac "woodies" were ordered from Hillcrest Cadillac, of Beverly Hills, by Hollywood's Metro-Goldwyn-Mayer studios. Whether the dealer or MGM itself was responsible for sending the cars to Maurice Schwartz for modification, we have been unable to ascertain.

In any event, most of the six employed

Cadillac's standard 136-inch, Series 75 wheelbase, though at least one was built on the 163-inch commercial chassis, more commonly used for ambulances and funeral coaches. According to one report, these glamorous Cadillacs "were used for transporting major stars to shooting locations within a convenient driving range." It seems more likely, however, that the Cadillacs were used to transport the more prominent support players, for it is reasonable to assume that those stars who rated top billing would have been driven in their own limousines.

Our driveReport car, a 1949 model, was the last of the six woodies to be built by Schwartz for MGM. It is believed to be the only survivor, and it, too, was very nearly lost. Reportedly, some time in the early 1950s it was driven to a photo location near Big Bear Lake, in the mountains 30 miles northeast of San Bernardino. There, under circumstances long forgotten, it was rolled, and ultimately abandoned. For something like ten or fifteen years, then, the Cadillac sat outdoors, its beautiful hardwood body rotting away under the relentless punishment of sun, rain, wind and snow.

Eventually the car was purchased by a collector named Dennis Mitosinka, who brought it back to Los Angeles, evidently intending to restore it. That would have been a horrendous undertaking, of course, and the work kept being postponed. Then in the early 1980s the Cad was purchased by a group of five Sacramento men headed

Above: Caddy exhibits superb wood construction. **Below left:** A Cadillac this deluxe would certainly have "sombrero" wheel covers. **Below right:** Sidelamps are nearly as large as the headlamps. **Bottom:** Wood adds sporty touch to a formal body style.

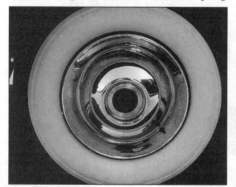

1949 CADILLAC

Above: Roof rack stanchions add to the chrome at the back of car. **Below left:** Compared to size of other lamps, reversing lamps are tiny. **Below right:** Cadillac's famous hidden gas filler first appeared on 1941 cars. **Bottom:** driveReport car wasn't always so glamourous. Here's how it looked after rollover and abandonment for 15 years.

by Al Robbins, a skilled wood artisan.

The men purchased a parts car, and restoration work got slowly under way. Using as much of the original wood as possible for patterns, Robbins was able to fabricate new ash framing and mahogany inserts, duplicating Maurice Schwartz's efforts. He did some badly needed metal work, rebuilt the roof rack, and repainted the car, substituting an attractive shade of red for the original black.

But one by one, as we understand the story, the five men in the consortium dropped away, until only Al Robbins was left, and Robbins was running out of money. By this time it was 1986 or early '87, at which point the Cadillac was purchased by Sacramento's Ramshead Collection. Much work remained to be done, a project undertaken by technician Bob Doyle and the rest of the Ramshead staff.

Al Robbins had done a fine job of refinishing the Cadillac's exterior; so no further work was undertaken in that area, except that all the brightwork had to be replated. The dash, however, had been painted black and cream, which did not harmonize well with the new body color; so it was refinished in a soft metallic beige. Running boards were

replaced, and a complete new interior was fitted, featuring the MGM logo on the assist straps and at the center of each rear door. Upholstery was done in Bedford cord with alligator trim, and hogshead carpeting was used, all in an effort to approximate the car's original elegance.

The mechanical restoration was similarly complete, including rebuilding the engine, HydraMatic transmission, and most of the remaining mechanical components. Some of this work was subbed out, but much of it was done on-site by members of the Ramshead staff.

By the time Metro-Goldwyn-Mayer purchased this magnificent automobile, Cadillac had come to dominate the market for long-wheelbase, limousine-type cars. The company built 1,501 Fleetwood Seventy-Fives during the 1949 model year, together with 1,861 163-inch commercial chassis. Chrysler, meanwhile, produced just 85 Crown Imperials that year.

Packard, which for many years had held the upper hand in this market, offered the largest engine in the group, a fine nine-bearing, flathead straight-eight displacing 356 cubic inches. But that year, Packard produced only 49 Custom Super Eights on the long, 148-inch chassis, before discontinuing production during May 1949. These cars, only an inch or so shorter than Chrysler's huge Crown Imperial, were rated, like Cadillac, at 160 horsepower, but the

Above: Cadillac's "flying lady" had become rather streamlined by 1949. *Below left:* Generous-sized heat outlets for passengers. *Below right:* Rear seat riders also had their own clock, of course. *Bottom:* Maurice Schwartz's famous shop, from which many custom creations emerged.

courtesy of Strother MacMinn

specifications

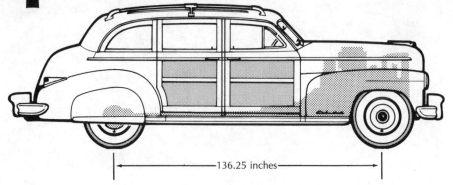 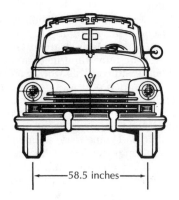

illustrations by Russell von Sauers, The Graphic Automobile Studio

© copyright 1994, Special Interest Autos

|←——— 136.25 inches ———→| |← 58.5 inches →|

1949 Cadillac Series 75

Original price $7,000 (est.)
Options HydraMatic transmission, power windows, power seat, white sidewall tires, "Sombrero" wheel covers, fender skirts, roof rack, radio, heater, backup lamp, left outside mirror

ENGINE
Type 90-degree overhead-valve V-8
Bore x stroke 3.8125 inches x 3.625 inches
Displacement 331.1 cubic inches
Compression ratio 7.5:1
Horsepower @ rpm 160 @ 3,800
Torque @ rpm 312 @ 1,800
Taxable horsepower 46.5
Valve lifters Hydraulic
Main bearings 5
Fuel system Carter 1.25-inch dual down-draft carburetor, camshaft pump
Lubrication system Pressure
Cooling system Centrifugal pump
Exhaust system Single
Electrical system Delco-Remy 6-volt battery/coil

TRANSMISSION
Type HydraMatic 4-speed automatic planetary
Ratios: 1st 3.82:1
2nd 2.63:1
3rd 1.45:1
4th 1.00:1
Reverse 4.31:1

DIFFERENTIAL
Type Hypoid
Ratio 3.77:1
Drive axles Semi-floating

STEERING
Type Saginaw recirculating ball
Turns lock-to-lock 4.75
Ratios 23.6:1
Turning diameter 48 feet 9 inches

BRAKES
Type Bendix 4-wheel hydraulic, drum type
Drum diameter 12 inches
Effective area 233 square inches
Braking distribution 56% front/44% rear

CHASSIS & BODY
Construction Body-on-frame
Frame Heavy channel iron, perimeter type with X-member
Body construction Steel with wood trim, wood doors
Coachbuilder Fleetwood body modified by Maurice Schwartz of Pasadena, California
Body type 8-passenger sedan

SUSPENSION
Front Independent coil and wishbone type
Rear Rigid axle, semi-elliptic springs
Shock absorbers Double-acting tubular type
Tires 7.50/16 6-ply
Wheels Pressed steel, drop-center rims

WEIGHTS AND MEASURES
Wheelbase 136.25 inches
Overall length 226 inches
Overall width 82.3125 inches
Overall height 68.5 inches (less roof rack)
Front track 58.5 inches
Rear track 62.5 inches
Min. road clearance 8.25 inches
Shipping weight 4,800 pounds (est.)

CAPACITIES
Crankcase 5 quarts
Cooling system 19 quarts (with heater)
Fuel tank 20 gallons
Transmission 21 pints
Rear axle 5 pints

CALCULATED DATA (based on estimated weight)
Horsepower per c.i.d. .483
Weight per hp 30.0 pounds
Weight per c.i.d. 14.5 pounds
PSI (brakes) 20.6 pounds
Speed per 1,000 rpm 23.25 mph (top gear)
Stroke/bore ratio 0.951:1

Right: Studio initials in door panels add true custom touch to interior. *Facing page, top:* A sports car it's not. Big limo hustles down road surprisingly swiftly but does tend to heel over in corners. *Center:* Luxury touches include smoking sets. *Bottom:* Instrument grouping is very well designed and convenient for driver.

1949 CADILLAC
continued

Cad held a significant advantage in torque: 312 versus the Packard's 282 foot-pounds.

There was, to be sure, another long-wheelbase Packard, and a fairly successful one. A member of the Super Eight series, this was a different class of automobile, probably intended primarily for the commercial trade. It had a much smaller, 327-c.i.d., five-bearing, 145-horsepower engine. Its eight-passenger models were built on a wheelbase of 141 inches, and they sold for as little as $3,950, more than a thousand dollars below the Cadillac and some $750 less than Packard's own Custom Super Eight.

During the years he spent with the Earl Carriage Works and Walter M. Murphy, Coachbuilders, as well as at Bohman and Schwartz, Maurice Schwartz must have modified any number of Packards. But by the time he built our driveReport car, Cadillac was clearly the car of choice, to provide the foundation for a prestige car such as this glamorous "woodie"!

Driving Impressions

That this is an ultra-luxury automobile goes without saying. There are clocks in both the front and rear compartments. (One has to wonder how they were kept coordinated, in those days before quartz timepieces were developed.) Both left and right armrests in the rear compartment are equipped with ashtrays and lighters. The center armrest is covered with alligator hide, and the fold-back footrest is deeply carpeted. Assist straps, which slide back and forth on metal rods, are augmented

Car of The Year!

There couldn't have been a great deal of debate when, in 1949, *Motor Trend* was preparing to designate its very first "Car of the Year." Only two manufacturers in those days were offering state-of-the-art engine design: Oldsmobile and Cadillac. For both had introduced, that season, highly efficient new short-stroke, overhead-valve V-8s. In contrast, every one of their American competitors still featured long-stroke powerplants whose origins dated from the 1930s, or even earlier. Most of the competition, in fact, continued to build side-valve engines, a configuration that had just about reached the limit of its potential.

As between Cadillac's new V-8 and that of sister-division Oldsmobile, the choice was clear. John Bond wrote at the time that "the engines are not by any means the same. The Cadillac, with ten percent more piston displacement, develops 18.5 percent more bhp and weighs a few pounds less."

Furthermore, there is evidence that the Cadillac design came first, and was influential in the development of the Olds "Rocket." Gilbert Burrell, who was largely responsible for the design of the Oldsmobile unit, has been quoted by auto journalist Jan P. Norbye as saying that "The Rocket was strictly an Oldsmobile project. I've been brought up to compete violently with other divisions."

But engineer Harry Barr, who was with Cadillac when the new V-8 was under development and later went on to become General Motors' engineering vice president, told a different story in a 1985 telephone interview with this writer. Barr explained that the development of the Cadillac engine commenced under the leadership of John F. "Jack" Gordon, who in later years became president of GM. But then Gordon was transferred to the Allison Division, where problems were being encountered with a new aircraft engine.

"This was just before we got into the war," Barr recalled, "'39 or '40. Then I took his [Gordon's] job as Motor Engineer [at Cadillac] and we were developing both an L-head and an overhead-valve engine, with the concept of a short stroke and a big bore. And we were going to see, by comparing these two engines that were identical in every [other] way, whether the L-head had a place with the higher compression ratios that we were going to have....

"We had these two engines just ready to go in dynamometer testing on December 7, 1941. Through the war years we got a lot of high-octane fuel, and we knew that the L-head could not make it; so we concentrated our efforts on the overhead valve. That was the genesis of the 1949 Cadillac. I was motor engineer on that, and Jack Gordon came back as chief engineer....

"Byron [Ellis] had gone to work on a better hydraulic [valve] lash adjuster for this new engine. We had a devil of a time with hydraulic lash adjusters on the tanks during the war. There were 16 of these things in a tank, under armor plate, and we couldn't get by the Army inspector if just one hydraulic tappet made a noise. They'd make a noise if a little chip of dirt got between the ball and the seat.... So Byron went to work to get a better hydraulic tappet. This was his assignment during the war. He came up with a very sharp radius and a hardened radius-seat to this ball. And that's the way all hydraulic lash-adjusters are made, post-war.

"So these things came together on the 1949 Cadillac engine, and we had a year's jump on anybody else.... There was a guy named C.L. McCuen, who had been general manager of Oldsmobile. He was vice president of the [GM] engineering staff, and knew all about our Cadillac engine because of his position. He convinced Jack [Gordon] that we should show this design to the Oldsmobile engineer. I well remember a guy by the name of Tony Waters, who was their engine-engineer, working with Jack Wilson. [He] came down and we showed him our entire design. And that's where Oldsmobile got started on what they tried to call the 'Kettering' engine. But [GM Chairman] Alfred Sloan said, 'You can't name an engine after a living individual,' so they changed it and called it the 'Rocket' engine.

"So Cadillac led that thing, I don't care what anybody says. We got into a cooperative program. We had some difficulty with tappet faces scoring the camshaft...and that's the one big contribution Oldsmobile made. They helped a lot in getting a durable tappet face, and got us out of that trouble."

One of the secrets of the new engine's lively performance lay in its unusual "slipper" pistons, another product of Byron Ellis's genius. A half-moon section, cut from either side of the lower skirt, permitted this piston to drop between the crankshaft counterweights. Thus shorter (and lighter) connecting rods could be employed, and the crankshaft weight was reduced by 30 pounds. Block, heads and crankcase were also reduced in weight, and the required cooling capacity was reduced. In the end the new engine was five inches shorter and four inches lower than the old L-head, and its "wet" weight (including radiator) was cut by 220 pounds.

The short-stroke design resulted in a 20 percent reduction in piston travel, from 3,000 to 2,400 feet per minute at 4,000 rpm. Friction was thus significantly reduced, resulting in longer engine life and improved fuel economy.

In the end, although the new engine's displacement was about four percent smaller than that of the old flathead, it provided Cadillac with a ten horsepower increase, along with a substantial advantage in fuel mileage. Zero-to-sixty time was cut by three seconds, and about six miles per hour was added to the top speed.

No wonder Cadillac was designated "Car of the Year."

1949 CADILLAC

by metal handles located adjacent to the doors. (We found those handles to be particularly useful, for getting out of that deeply padded rear seat can be something of a struggle.)

1949 was, of course, the first year for Cadillac's sensational new overhead-valve V-8, which supplied ten more horsepower and 29 additional foot pounds of torque, compared to the venerable flathead of earlier years. (See sidebar, page 68.) Nevertheless, given its considerable weight, we expected the big Cadillac to be rather a slug. So we were pleasantly surprised to find that it gets off the line in fairly sprightly fashion. Acceleration at passing speeds could hardly be called flashy, but we found it to be entirely adequate. The car cruises quietly and smoothly at maximum permissible freeway speeds, and even a little beyond.

The HydraMatic transmission was supplied as standard issue on the 1949 Series Sixty-Two and Sixty-Special Cadillacs, but it was a $174 option on the Fleetwood Seventy-Fives, as well as the price-leading Series Sixty-Ones. (Presumably, in the case of the big Fleetwoods, the thinking was that the owner-drivers would prefer the automatic, but the hired chauffeurs, who often drove the larger machines, could jolly well shift for themselves.) Like all the early HydraMatics, this one produces a pronounced surge when shifting from first to second gear, but otherwise it works smoothly, and with less slippage than one might anticipate.

Suspension is on the soft side, though the ride is not quite as spongy as some Buicks of the same era. There's stretch-

Facing page: Another of the six Schwartz-built Cadillac woodies. Wood treatment on rear quarters is different from driveReport car. **This page, above:** *First-year ohw V-8 provides noticeably more punch than its flathead predecessor.* **Below:** *Alligator hide and fine broadcloth is used throughout the interior.* **Bottom:** *King of the Schwartz Caddy woodies was this gargantuan six-door job built for carrying a bevy of MGM starlets.*

1949 CADILLAC

out leg room front and rear, of course, and we found the Cadillac to be — as expected — exceptionally comfortable. It does heel over rather sharply in hard cornering, however.

Power steering had not yet made its appearance in 1949; so it came as no surprise to find that it takes a bit of muscle to turn the wheel in this big car. Brakes, also without power-assist, do their work very well, and with less pedal pressure than we expected.

It happened that there was a 1948 Chrysler Crown Imperial at the Ramshead Collection when we visited there; so we were able to take it out for a brief comparison drive. This is an enormous automobile, nine inches longer, even, than the big Cadillac. Accordingly, leg room is even more generous in the Chrysler than in the Cad. Like our driveReport car, the Crown Imperial offers a superb ride. It corners a little flatter than the Cadillac, and it steers much easier, we found.

In terms of acceleration, however, it's the Cadillac's game all the way. Weight of the two cars is nearly identical, but the Cad enjoys a distinct advantage in

Table of Prices, Weights and Production

	Price	Weight	Production
Series 61: 129-inch WB			
Club Coupe	$2,788	3,838 lb.	6,409
Sedan, 4-door	$2,893	3,915 lb.	15,738
Chassis only	N/A	N/A	1
Total production, Series 61			22,148
Series 62: 129-inch WB			
Club Coupe	$2,966	3,862 lb.	7,515
Sedan, 4-door	$3,050	3,956 lb.	37,617
Convertible Coupe	$3,497	4,218 lb.	8,000
Coupe de Ville (hdtp)	$3,496	4,033 lb.	2,150
Export Sedan, 4-door	$3,050	3,956	360
Chassis only	N/A	N/A	1
Total production, Series 62			55,643
Series 60 Special Fleetwood: 133-inch WB			
Sedan, 4-door	$3,828	4,129	11,399
Special Coupe de Ville	N/A	N/A	1
Total Production, Series 60-Special Fleetwood			11,400
Series 75 Fleetwood: 136.25-inch WB			
Sedan, 4-door, 5-passenger	$4,750	4,570 lb.	220
Sedan, 4-door, 7-passenger	$4,970	4,625 lb.	595
Imperial Sedan, 7-passenger	$5,170	4,648	626
Business Sedan, 9-passenger	$4,650	4,522 lb.	35
Business Imperial, 9-passenger	$4,839	4,573 lb.	25
Chassis only	N/A	N/A	1*
Commercial Chassis (163-inch WB)	N/A	N/A	1,861

* Presumably this was the chassis used for our driveReport car

Total production, Series 75 Fleetwood	3,363
Grand total, 1949 model year production	92,554
Total 1949 calendar year production	81,545

1949 CADILLAC

continued from page 71

Left: Maurice Schwartz at work in his wood shop. Below: Schwartz innovations included this pillarless invalid car. Bottom: Caddy woodie is absolutely massive in appearance!

horsepower (160 vs. 135) and torque (312 vs. 270 foot pounds). In combination with the greater efficiency of the HydraMatic transmission, as compared to Chrysler's M-6 PrestoMatic, those differences — which amount to 18.5 and 15.6 percent, respectively — make the Cadillac seem almost like a muscle car compared to the Imperial. ❏

Acknowledgements and Bibliography

Automotive Industries, *March 15 and June 1, 1949*; Bond, John, *"Car of the Year: The 1949 Cadillac," Motor Trend, November 1949*; Hendry, Maurice D., *Cadillac: The Complete History*; Langworth, Richard M., *Encyclopedia of American Cars, 1940-1970*; McCall, Walter M.P., *80 Years of Cadillac-LaSalle*; MacMinn, Strother, *"The Lighter Side of Bohman & Schwartz,"* Special Interest Autos #11, *June/July 1972*; Schneider, Roy A., *Cadillacs of the Forties*; *"The High-Compression Cadillacs," Motor, March 2, 1949.*

Our thanks to Bob Doyle, Sacramento, California; Strother MacMinn, Pasadena, California; Carl Steig, San Leandro, California; Bob Weiss, Stockton, California. Special thanks to The Ramshead Collection, Sacramento, California.

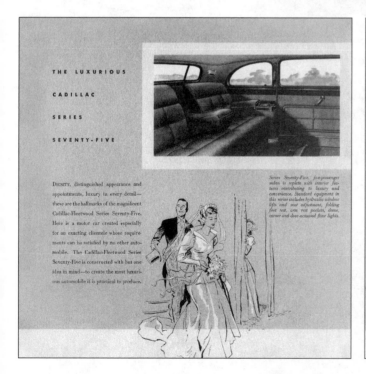

1953/59 Cadillac LeMans

by Tim Howley
photos by David Gooley

OUR driveReport car is Cadillac's star of the 1953 GM Motorama, one of four such cars built, one of three known to survive. It is LeMans #4, built for J.E. "Bud" Goodman, then head of GM's Fisher Body Division, and still owned by his son Jack after 45 years. This particular LeMans was returned to GM styling in 1959, where it was facelifted and outfitted with a 1959 Cadillac engine and HydraMatic transmission. The car is all original to its 1959 facelift, and at the time of our road test had 18,635 original miles. We discovered this car in the basement/garage of the Petersen Museum in Los Angeles when we were developing our article on original cars in the Petersen Museum (see *SIA* #166, August 1998).

Normally, these concept/show cars do not ride or handle nearly as well as the production cars. Most are pretty tinny because they are built for show, not for go. This is not true of the LeMans. It has more of the characteristics of a production car than a show car.

Said *Motor Trend* of the LeMans when they drove one at the GM Proving Grounds, it has "moderately sensitive steering and good road-holding, but definitely [is] too heavy and spongy for competition." The LeMans had an all-fiberglass body and 115-inch wheelbase (11 inches less than the 1953 Cadillac) and was 400 pounds lighter than a 1953 Cadillac convertible. The original engine developed 250 horsepower and had 9:1 compression ratio. A standard 1953 Cadillac developed 210 horsepower and had 8.25:1 compression ratio. This car has the 1959 Cadillac Eldorado engine with 345 horsepower and 10.5:1 compression ratio, fed by triple two-barrel carburetors, which was a feature of this engine.

Our impression of the car is that it had very similar handling and ride to the 1954-55 Cadillac, but with all the wallop of the '59 Eldorado engine. Its roadability is good, but there is nothing that would put it in the sports car class.

Originally published in Special Interest Autos #169, Jan.-Feb. 1999

This is due in part to suspension, in part to power steering, and in part to its sheer bulkiness, although the car has considerably less weight and size than a standard 1953 or '54 Cadillac convertible. It takes dips, bumps and pot holes with little discomfort. It is not as mushy as pre-1954 Cadillacs and has a definite edge over the standard '53 in stability. Choppy road surfaces are soaked up easily in the car's suspension, but there is more road noise than other Cadillacs of the period. It is a heavy car, and you can sense its weight in the handling and ride. You would think the fiberglass would make it feel lighter, but it doesn't.

Like any Cadillac, it is hard to criticize on the basis of handling ease. The easy-turning steering system has a near total lack of feel, something we criticize in all Cadillacs of the fifties. Braking is good by 1954 luxury car standards, although a little abrupt and is a far cry from that of power front disc brake luxury cars of a decade or so later.

We were most disappointed in the instrumentation which was done up in special Harley Earl Motorama glitz and was even harder to read than standard Cadillacs of the period. The instrument panel is totally unique to the LeMans with two big instrument pods containing the tachometer and speedometer and smaller ones containing fuel, signal seeking radio, temperature, battery and oil and, finally, the clock to the far right. The driver either needs to be a giraffe or have a co-pilot to read all of the instruments. The instrument faces themselves are not easy to read, with white numerals on a silver field. They look like something that might have been designed for a forties Buick. We got the feeling that

Harley Earl was still clinging to the Buick Y-Job (see *SIA* #157) when this car's instrumentation was designed, but the 1938 Y-Job had a better instrument layout than the LeMans. The glove box is completely concealed at the far right

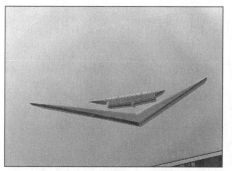

under the dash. It is a drawer that drops down at the passenger's feet. There are three rear-view mirrors, dash-mounted and left and right outside, all so small that only Snow White's Seven Dwarfs can see into them. They rather remind

*Top: There are plenty of styling clues for Cadillacs to come in the LeMans design. **Above left:** Traditional V and crest adorn trunk lid. **Right:** Only four cars ever wore this particular script. **Below:** Taillamp treatment points directly toward Eldo Brougham styling.*

Left: *Turbine-blade wheels also became a Caddy trademark.* **Right:** *Front bumper and grille are from '55 and '54 Cadillacs respectively. They were updated from original front end years ago.*

Cadillac LeMans

us of the tiny mirrors used by dentists. The brake pedal is also elf size. These are some of the silly things characteristically found on show cars. We liked the HydraMatic quadrant on the instrument panel, not the steering column, but we disliked the setup. Park is at the left and reverse is at the right, meaning when you start out in your garage and back out you have to go all the way through neutral, D2, D1 and low to reach reverse, which was the typical awkward shifting setup for all Cadillacs of this vintage.

Other novelties are push-button doors, a two-way power seat with a near impossible-to-find control on the seat under the driver. It is two-way only, and the seat retracts automatically when the door is opened, then moves back to a preset memory position when the door is closed. The seat is bench style, not bucket style. The heater/defroster/fresh air controls are aircraft-style levers. Oddly, the car does not have air-conditioning, which was a much-touted Cadillac option at the time. The battery is at the forward end of the trunk, and the trunk has two handles instead of one. The backup lights are in the exhaust pods. This car has Cadillac's first signal-seeking radio, and the

antenna goes up automatically when the radio is turned on.

Cadillac never seriously considered putting the LeMans into limited production, although dealers claimed there was a market for 5,000 of them. Had it ever been produced in those numbers, it might have had a $10,000 price tag which, like the 1956 Continental Mark II, would have meant that the market would have been limited to the Rockefellers, Clark Gable, Joe DiMaggio and a few others of that ilk and era. Remember, 1953 was the year that Cadillac did introduce the limited production Eldorado convertible, which had a base price of $7,750 and only 553 were produced. Perhaps the Eldorado and its limited success in the marketplace kept Cadillac from producing more than four LeMans.

Our driveReport car was built especially for J.E. "Bud" Goodman. It is doubtful that it ever went on the Cadillac show circuit. Goodman was a close friend of Harley Earl, and Earl was delighted to build one just for him. Son Jack is uncertain of the car's complete story. When Jack moved to the Los Angeles area in 1960 he bought into and eventually owned Dixon Cadillac in Hollywood. (Can you imagine all the movie stars that walked through those doors!) The car was on display in the dealership for years. When Goodman sold the dealership, he moved the car into his Beverly Hills garage. The car presently is on loan to the Petersen Museum in Los Angeles. When not on display it resides in the Petersen Museum underground garage.

Down through the years, the car has required virtually no maintenance other than such routine chores as mufflers, tires, batteries and tuneups. Jack has never had to go through the engine,

Barris LeMans

The third LeMans was customized (some would say ruined) by customizer George Barris, then located in Lynwood, California. This car was owned by Harry Karl, Los Angeles shoe store magnate, who at one time was married to Debbie Reynolds.

Barris left the body fiberglass except for his addition of lower fender panels, which were formed of body steel, then bluewhite chrome plated. Trim between the lower chromed parts of the fenders and the fiberglass part of the body was a half-inch steel bar, plated with 24-karat gold. To stop rattles, a strip of 1/8-inch rubber separated the gold-plated trim from the body panels. The upper rear fender panels were covered in stainless steel to simulate exaggerated tail fins. A continental kit was integrated into the rear deck. Hubcaps were done in a combination of gold and chrome, then 30 individually inserted spokes were added, plus a protruding center of gold. The remainder was in chrome. The paint was 30 coats of "platinum dust."

Barris added a top to this car, which had a huge glass or Plexiglas bubble rear window. The rear window and the top were trimmed with chrome-plated steel. The top was completely removable, or the rear window could be left in place with the rest of the top removed.

The car, as customized by Barris, had a television set, radio-telephone, tape recorder and cocktail bar in the rear window area. The bar was hidden under a red leather panel which matched the upholstery.

The engine was a 300-horsepower Cadillac with dual four-barrel carburetors as originally equipped by the factory. All engine accessories, valve covers, etc, were chrome plated per the factory.

Barris was famous for doing customs like this at the time for movie stars, celebrities and Los Angeles executives who liked to flaunt their success. While the Barris customization of this car added nothing to the original clean styling of the LeMans, it certainly gave this one a place in history.

transmission or suspension, a testimony to Cadillac's fine engineering in the fifties. We have received similar satisfactory reports from owners of production Cadillacs of the same period. Since all the mechanical components are standard Cadillac, either 1953 or 1959, they are not difficult to find. Body, body trim, and interior trim are something else. All body and most trim pieces are customized to the car except for the 1954 grille and 1955 front bumper assembly. Even a minor accident in this car would be a nightmare, one more reason why the car is seldom driven. At the time the car was built, two extra windshields were molded. Goodman still has them both, never out of the crates.

In the early fifties Harley Earl went wraparound, or panoramic, windshield crazy. When Earl went to Libby-Owens-Ford to have them built, they told GM that Earl was plumb nuts. Earl told them to build such windshields anyway, and they did. If he had asked for an all-glass car they would have built it. Such was the power that this man possessed. The panoramic windshield on the LeMans is unique to these cars. It is also canted back. Standard Cadillac windshields had perfectly vertical A pillars and were not canted back until 1957.

The 1953 Cadillac LeMans

Dave Holls, who came into Cadillac styling just at the end of the LeMans project, remembers how the car came to be styled. Holls worked on the instrument panel, but not the entire car. The LeMans was done under Ed Glowacke,

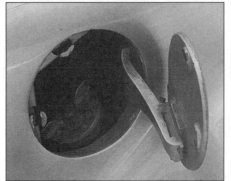

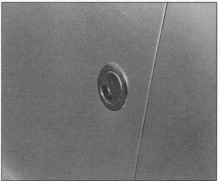

Top: Low, aggressive stance gives front a strong visual impression. **Center:** Hidden fuel filler on inside of left fender fin, push-button doors help keep body sides flush. **Above:** "Airscoops" help break up large expanse of sheet metal on rear fender areas.

illustrations by Russell von Sauers, The Graphic Automobile Studio

specifications

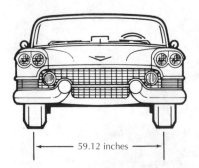

59.12 inches

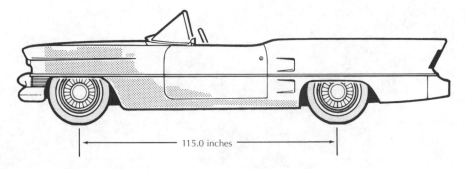

115.0 inches

1953/59 Cadillac LeMans two-door sports roadster

Standard equipment HydraMatic, power steering, power brakes, power windows, power seat, signal-seeking radio, whitewall tires

ENGINE
Type	Ohv V-8
Bore x stroke	4 inches x 3.875 inches
Displacement	390 cubic inches
Compression ratio	10.5:1
Horsepower @ rpm	345 @ 4,800
Torque @ rpm	435 @ 3,400
Induction system	Triple 2-barrel carburetor
Exhaust system	Cast-iron manifolds, dual exhausts
Electrical system	6-volt battery/coil

TRANSMISSION
Type	HydraMatic
Ratios: 1st	3.97:1
2nd	2.55:1
3rd	1.55:1
Reverse	3.74:1

DIFFERENTIAL
Type	Hotchkiss

Ratio	3.07:1
Drive axles	Semi-floating

STEERING
Type	Recirculating ball
Turns lock-to-lock	5
Ratio	25:1
Turning circle	21 feet

BRAKES
Type	4-wheel hydraulic drum
Drum diameter	12 inches
Total swept area	258 square inches

CHASSIS & BODY
Frame	Channel-section steel, double-dropped, central X member, reinforced
Body construction	All fiberglass
Body style	Roadster with roll-up windows

SUSPENSION
Front	Independent A-arm, coil springs, tubular double-acting hydraulic shocks
Rear	Semi-elliptic leaf springs, tubular double-acting hydraulic shocks
Tires	9.15 x 15

WEIGHTS AND MEASURES
Wheelbase	115 inches
Overall length	196 inches
Overall width	80 inches
Overall height	51 inches
Front track	59.12 inches
Rear track	63 inches
Shipping weight	4,076 pounds (approximately)

CAPACITIES
Crankcase	6 quarts (including filter)
Cooling system	19.7 quarts
Fuel tank	17.6 gallons
Transmission	23 pints

FUEL CONSUMPTION
Average city driving	13 mpg
Avg. open road driving	17 mpg

Right: By 1953, wraparound windshields had already appeared on limited-production Eldorados and Olds Fiestas, but they didn't have the extreme rake of LeMans's windshield. *Facing page, top:* For softly sprung car, LeMans has good roadholding. *Center left:* Spare is recessed into trunk floor. *Right:* When's the last time you saw a chromed bumper jack? *Bottom left:* Exhuast pod styling says nothing but "Cadillac." *Right:* Original engine has been replaced by monster '59 Eldorado V-8, making the LeMans a show car that's also a go-car.

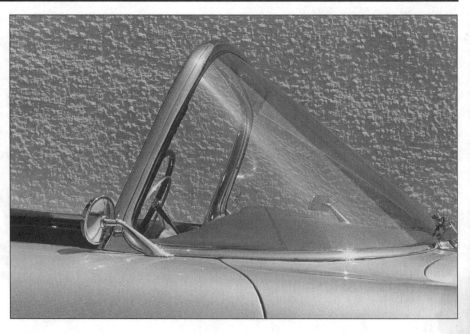

Cadillac LeMans

who took over the Cadillac styling studio in 1951. In the early fifties Cadillacs had a very heavy look, especially the grille. With the LeMans, they were trying to get away from that look. The LeMans was a very light looking car with a rather delicate grille, reminiscent of the 1941 Cadillac. With this car Harley Earl was able to sell management on the 1954 Cadillac design. Even though it accurately predicted 1954 production Cadillac styling, GM decided to put it in their

1954 Motorama anyway. At the time they were giving away their styling secrets, one reason why the Motoramas were eventually discontinued.

The Cadillac LeMans was named for the famous 24-hour road race. (Briggs

Cunningham participated in the 1950 LeMans race with a basically stock 1950 Cadillac Coupe de Ville and the Cadillac-powered "Le Monstre." Also, a Cadillac engine powered the J2 Allard, which finished third in the 1950

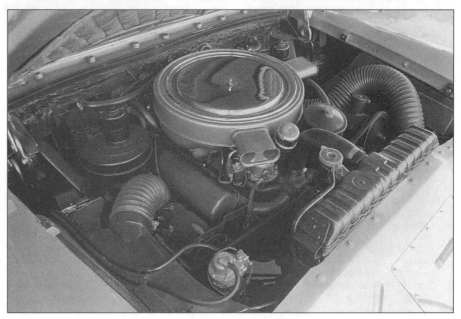

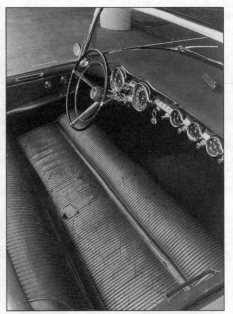

Left: *Speedo and tach are custom units presented in the sports car mode of white on black.* ***Right:*** *Fine custom leatherwork makes a sumptuous bench seat. It now needs restoration.*

Cadillac LeMans

LeMans race. Additionally, the Cunningham C-3 sports car was powered by a Cadillac engine.)

The original LeMans show car was a silver-blue fiberglass car. Like our driveReport LeMans, it had a 115-inch wheelbase, stood 51 inches and was 196 inches overall. It was powered by a 250-horsepower Cadillac ohv V-8, coupled to a HydraMatic transmission adapted to the increased engine output. The engine was painted a silver-blue and trimmed with chrome to match the car.

The grille and front bumper looked the same as the 1954 Cadillac, but there are subtle differences. For instance, the outer area, which wraps around to the front wheel well, is different from the production model. The entire front clip has the same styling as that of the 1954 Cadillac. Body side panels, side trim and tail fins all accurately predict 1954 Cadillac styling. Given all the 1954 Cadillac styling cues, it is a mystery why the LeMans did not have a 1954 Cadillac instrument panel. Incidentally, and for reasons we cannot explain, the Goodman car has what appears to be a 1955 Cadillac front bumper, which is slightly different than the 1954.

The rear bumper, except for the end pods, was made up of vertical strips of steel. They appeared to be part of the body design but were internally braced and were capable of withstanding shock the same as a conventional rear bumper. The instrument panel was the same as the one in the Goodman car. The HydraMatic indicator was moved from the steering column into the instrument panel. This did not appear on production models until 1954.

Leather workers from England embossed the Cadillac V and crest into the fine leather of the seat back, and jewelers fashioned the hand-engraved surfaces of the hood emblem, the LeMans script on the wheel discs and the lettering on the instrument panel. As an extension of these artistic refinements, the carpeting was a specially created nylon needlepoint. Upholstery of the LeMans was hand buffed leather of a matching silver-blue. The bolster at the forward edge of the seat contained a tube for umbrella storage with a chromed cap carrying the LeMans insigne.

When lowered, the silver-blue Orlon top was recessed in the rear deck and covered by a fiberglass boot. In addition

Other Cadillac Show Cars of the Period

Orleans

Accompanying the LeMans to the 1953 Motorama was the Orleans, derived from a 1953 Series 62 two-door hardtop. It was America's first pillarless four-door hardtop. GM later introduced four-door hardtops on all makes, starting with Oldsmobile in 1955, and all other makes in 1956. There is no explanation as to why Cadillac did not introduce four-door hardtops earlier than 1956 or why they did not name all their four-door hardtops "Orleans."

El Camino

This 1954 show car with aircraft styling and 1957 Cadillac fins had a 115-inch wheelbase and 230-horsepower 1954 Cadillac engine. Overall length was 200.6 inches, height was 51.1 inches. The El Camino was not a convertible, nor did it have a removable hardtop. It had a permanent domelike top. The windshield had a rear-canted A pillar and the rear window had a forward-canted C pillar. The car offered many styling cues for the 1957-58 production Cadillacs. Painted silver-gray, the El Camino had a brushed aluminum roof top coated with clear lacquer, a tinted glass panoramic windshield, twin taillights with side slots and a keel below the taillamps, again a 1957 Cadillac touch. Horizontal flutes swept along the sides of the front fenders. The El Camino had four hooded headlights in the front fenders.

The front bumper had massive Dagmars.

Inside there was a cluster of instruments around the steering column. Between two leather-covered seats was a tunnel housing the HydraMatic gearshift selector. The setup was very similar to the 1963 Buick Riviera. Behind the gear lever was a radio and vanity compartment. Heater and air conditioning controls were forward of the gear lever. The El Camino was designed by Dave Holls.

La Espada

La Espada was a fiberglass experimental convertible finished in metallic gold and trimmed with chrome and aluminum. It had a high luster black leather and brushed aluminum interior. Wheelbase was 115 inches; overall length was 200.6 inches. The engine was the 1954 Cadillac 230-horsepower V-8.

Park Avenue

The Park Avenue was the prelude to the Cadillac Eldorado Brougham and 1957-58 Cadillac four-doors. It was a four-door sedan with frames around the side windows, not a four-door hardtop. The Park Avenue was constructed of fiberglass, and was far more restrained in design than the roadsters. The exterior color was dark blue, trimmed with chrome, and the top was hand-brushed aluminum. The engine was the 1954 Cadillac 230-horsepower V-8.

to a manually operated control, the top was also automatically actuated by a rain switch to raise if the car was exposed to a sudden shower. The Goodman car does not have this rain switch feature.

The wheels were distinguished by chromed blades radiating from the hub—a design inspired by the appearance of aircraft turbines.

Cadillac never intended to put the LeMans into production. It was strictly a

concept car. Somehow four were built, Holls is not sure why. GM did some strange things in those days. The original one, which appeared in the 1953 Motorama, has disappeared; its present owner and location are unknown, if, indeed it still exists. The second one was sold new to Floyd Acres, who was the Cadillac dealer in Washington, DC. The car was intended for Acres's daughter, but when the dealership was sold the car inadvertently went with the deal, so the family lost it. In 1989 the car was sold privately for $350,000. It went to an individual who did not want to be named. Its present whereabouts is un-

known. The third one was sold to Southern California shoe store owner Harry Karl, who had George Barris customize it, and then displayed it on a trailer in front of his shoe stores. (see sidebar, page 72.) This car is now owned by Jack Posey. It was later partially destroyed in a fire, but still exists. The fourth LeMans is the one featured in this article.

In 1959, this car went back into GM or Cadillac styling. The color was changed from a metallic sea mist green to silver inside and out. The hood was lowered. A new, low-profile Harrison radiator was added. The front went from single to

Remembering Mid-Fifties Cadillacs

I'm sorry to say that as a teenager I never knew anybody who had a Cadillac from the early to mid-fifties. They were just way out of the reach of almost everybody in Forest Lake, Minnesota, where I went to high school. In 1958, when I was a radio announcer at KSUM in Fairmont, Minnesota, the station owner had a lavender 1957 Cadillac Coupe de Ville. I guess that for what little he paid me he could afford it. About 25 years ago, living in San Rafael, California, I picked up a gold and white Cadillac Coupe de Ville. It was a fine, original, one-owner car for which I paid $900. After owning it for a short period, I came to discover that the 96,000 miles was more like 196,000 miles. The car required a complete mechanical rebuild. So I bailed out of it and barely got my $900 investment back. Such were the prices of fifties Cadillacs back then. The car went up to Oregon and that was the last I heard of it. How I would love to have a 1955 Cadillac now, my favorite Cadillac year. It would fit nicely between my 1954 Chrysler and 1956 Lincoln. There is something about the baroque styling of these Cadillacs that has always fascinated me.

*Top: Remainder of gauges are surrounded by chrome and spread across dashboard. They look great but are difficult for driver to scan. **Above:** Special LeMans badges were designed for the four cars, combining Cadillac crest with the model's name.*

Top left: Lowness of body is emphasized by fins. Maximum height is a bit over four feet. *Right:* Low-revving V-8 develops peak horses at 4,800 rpm. *Below left:* First owner's initials are engraved in wheel hub. *Right:* Hinged glove box slides out for easy access.

Cadillac LeMans

dual headlights. The fins were streamlined and the gas filler cap in the fin was eliminated. The air ducts in the rear quarters were changed. The original 331-c.i.d. engine was exchanged for the most powerful new 390 and a matching transmission. The original, removable fiberglass hardtop was discarded, probably because

Mr. Goodman never used it. This facelift was Harley Earl's idea. Bud Goodman never asked that it be done. Earl just wanted to update the car for his friend and for his own personal satisfaction.

Jack's father seldom drove the car. As a kid in college, Jack drove the car around Birmingham, Michigan. Jack came to California in 1960. When he took over Dixon Cadillac in 1963, his father had the car shipped to California for Jack's personal use at the dealership.

There is a great story about when

Clubs and Specialists

Cadillac-LaSalle Club, Inc.
PO Box 1916
Lenoir, NC 28645-1916
828-757-9919; 828-757-0367 FAX
E-mail:cadlasal@twave.net
For Cadillac and LaSalle collectors and enthusiasts. 6,200 members with regions in 23 states.

Postwar Cadillac specialists:

Ed Cholakian Enterprises, Inc.
12811 Foothill Blvd.
Sylmar, CA 91342
800-808-1147; 818-361-1147
818-361-9738 FAX
Specializing in Cadillac parts from 1940 to 1958.

Holcombe Cadillac Parts
2933 Century Lane
Bensalem, PA 19020
215-245-4560; 215-633-9916 FAX
Specializing in Cadillac parts from 1949 to 1983.

Justin Hartley
17 Fox Meadow Lane
West Hartford, CT 06107-1216
860-523-0056; 860-604-9950 cellular
860-233-8840 FAX
Specializing in reprinted Cadillac shop manuals for all years through 1995.

Harley Earl returned to Styling after the LeMans was first shown to the public at the Motorama. Dave Holls recalls Earl telling everyone about the reaction to the LeMans. "They loved that car," Earl said. "You know who loved the LeMans the most? John Wayne! He wants one. I told him it was a show car and we couldn't build one just for him. I told him it was built out of fiberglass. Wayne said, 'I don't care if it's built out of puddin', I want one'."

There is no explanation why one was not built for John Wayne. It is entirely possible that the first one, which has disappeared, went to Wayne, but any records have been lost. Up until that time GM sold many of their concept cars. But they were not up to GM quality standards. They rattled and rumbled and parts would fall off. The buyers would then complain. So after 1953 GM had a policy of destroying these cars, although a few have survived in collections like that of Joe Bortz. ❧

Acknowledgments and Bibliography

"Cadillac, The Complete 70-Year History," Maurice D. Hendry, Automobile Quarterly, 1973; *"Cars of Today,"* Speed Age, 1953; *"GM's Nine Cars of Tomorrow,"* Motor Life, April 1954; *"1953 Cadillac, America's Favorite Luxury Car,"* Walt Woron and Pete Molson, Motor Trend, May 1953; *"1954 Cadillac,"* Jim Lodge, Motor Trend, July 1954; *"LeMans, A Barris Bonanza,"* Bill Babbitt, Motor Trend, December 1955.

Special thanks to owner Jack Goodman, Beverly Hills, California; the Petersen Museum, Los Angeles, California; and Dave Holls, Detroit, Michigan.

The GM Motoramas

The GM Motoramas, grandest, gaudiest and giddiest of all the fifties car shows, were rooted in Alfred P. Sloan's luncheons at the Waldorf-Astoria, dating back to 1931. After World War II, GM decided to expand the Waldorf affairs and open them up to the public. The first Motorama, which was called "Transportation Unlimited," was held in the Waldorf's grand ballroom in January 1949. Added to the cars was a stage revue with orchestra, singers and dancers.

The Motoramas were mainly the creation of Harley Earl, who was always more showman than practical designer. He saw the extravaganzas as an opportunity to excite the buying public for cars to come and also test their reaction to his newest ideas, many quite radical.

The 1953 Motorama was probably the most historic of all because it introduced so many new cars and new ideas—including the 1953 Corvette. In fact, the name Motorama was introduced in 1953 when these shows began traveling around the country. Each Motorama ran for nine days, a week with a weekend at each end. They were held through 1961, but not in all years (see accompanying chart).

What happened to the Motoramas? After 1961, GM turned its show efforts towards the 1964 New York World's Fair. Then, in the mid-sixties, television made Motoramas financially impractical, as TV specials drew larger audiences for less money. Another reason was that GM felt it was giving away its secrets to the competition.

However, GM continued to build dream cars for the various auto shows around the country. For the full story of the Motoramas, see *Special Interest Autos* #21, March-April 1974.

Motorama Years

Year	Where held
1949	New York, Boston
1950	New York
1953	New York, Miami, Los Angeles, San Francisco, Dallas, Kansas City
1954	New York, Miami, Los Angeles, San Francisco, Chicago
1955	New York, Miami, Los Angeles, San Francisco, Boston
1956	(same as above)
1959	New York, Boston
1961	New York, San Francisco, Los Angeles

Note: GM Motoramas were held only in the eight years listed. Source: General Motors Corp.

The Compleat Eldorado Spotters Guide

BY JEFF GODSHALL

1953 ELDORADO:
- DROPPED DOOR LINE
- PANORAMIC WINDSHIELD
- DISAPPEARING TOP WITH METAL COVER
- FOUR BODY COLORS
- WIRE WHEELS & WSW TIRES
- PRICED @ $7750

1954 ELDORADO:
- ALL NEW BODY W/PANORAMIC WINDSHIELD
- CELLULAR EGG-CRATE GRILLE
- FOUR SPECIAL BODY COLORS
- FIBERGLASS CONVERTIBLE TOP COVER

1954 ELDORADO:
- SPECIAL RIBBED BRIGHT APPLIQUÉ ON REAR FENDERS
- GOLD CRESTS ON DOOR & REAR FENDER
- WIRE WHEELS & WSW TIRES
- PRICED @ $5738

1955 ELDORADO:
- NEW GRILLE WITH WIDER SPACING OF DAGMAR BUMPER GUARDS
- PARK & TURN LIGHTS UNDER HEADLIGHTS

1955 ELDORADO:
- NEW BACK END WITH FINS & FAIRED-IN TAILLIGHTS
- SIX VERTICAL CHROME BARS ABOVE BUMPER
- NEW SIDE MOLDING
- RIBBED BRIGHT TRIM AT BELT
- SABRE-SPOKE WHEELS & WSW TIRES
- PRICED @ $6286

GODSHALL '74

1956 ELDORADO:
- NEW FINER EGG-CRATE GRILLE
- DOUBLE FIN HOOD ORNAMENT
- GRILLE AVAILABLE IN BRIGHT OR GOLD FINISH
- NEW REAR BUMPER W/LICENSE PLATE IN BUMPER

1956 ELDORADO SEVILLE:
- NEW HARDTOP MODEL — CONVERTIBLE NAMED 'BIARRITZ'
- FABRIC-FINISH ROOF ON SEVILLE
- SABRE-SPOKE WHEELS IN BRIGHT OR GOLD FINISH— WSW TIRES
- BRIGHT RIBBED TRIM AT BELT
- PRICED @ $6556

1957 ELDORADO BIARRITZ:
- ALL NEW BODY STYLING
- UNIQUE 'CHIPMUNK CHEEK' REAR QUARTER PANELS
- SLOPING DECK WITH SMALL FINS
- SEVILLE HARDTOP WITH FABRIC-FINISH ROOF
- SABRE-SPOKE WHEELS IN BRIGHT OR GOLD FINISH— WSW TIRES

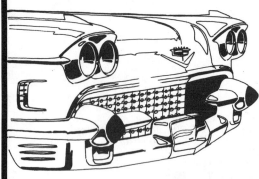

1958 ELDORADO:
- NEW FRONT END STYLING
- 'BULLET EGG CRATE GRILLE IN BRIGHT OR GOLD
- CHROME MOLDING ON FENDER & DOOR
- TEN LOUVRES ON REAR QUARTER
- NEW REAR BUMPER STYLING WITH BIGGER BACK-UP LAMPS
- FIVE LOUVRES ON EACH SIDE OF LICENSE PLATE
- SABRE-SPOKE WHEELS —WSW TIRES
- BIARRITZ & SEVILLE MODELS PRICED @ $7500

1957 ELDORADO:
- GULL-WING DAGMARS W/RUBBER TIPS
- EGG-CRATE GRILLE
- DUAL FENDER ORNAMENTS
- PRICED @ $7286
- BRIGHT OR GOLD GRILLE

GODSHALL '74

1959 ELDORADO SEVILLE:
- ALL NEW BODY WITH WILDEST-EVER FINS & ROCKET TAILLIGHTS
- SPECIAL BODY SIDE MOLDING FOLLOWING BODY CONTOURS
- SPECIAL REAR COVE GRILLE - 'V' CREST OVER BACK-UP LIGHTS
- SPECIAL WHEEL COVERS - WSW TIRES
- NEW FRONT END WITHOUT DAGMARS
- 'BULLET' EGG-CRATE GRILLE
- SEVILLE & BIARRITZ MODELS PRICED @ $ 7401

1960 ELDORADO:
- NEW SIMPLER 'BULLET' EGG-CRATE GRILLE
- NEW BUMPER W/SQUARE PARK & TURN LAMPS

1960 ELDORADO:
- NEW REAR STYLING WITH LOWER FINS & OVAL BUMPER ENDS
- SPECIAL REAR GRILLE MATCHING FRONT GRILLE
- SPECIAL BODY SIDE MOLDINGS FOLLOWING BODY CONTOURS
- SPECIAL WHEEL COVERS - WSW TIRES
  BIARRITZ & SEVILLE MODELS
  PRICED @ $ 7401

1961 ELDORADO BIARRITZ:
- ALL NEW STYLING WITH LOWER SKEG FIN
- SPECIAL BODY SIDE MOLDING ON UPPER CHARACTER LINE
- BODY-COLOR WHEEL COVERS - WSW TIRES
- CONVERTIBLE MODEL ONLY PRICED @ $ 6477

GODSHALL '74

81

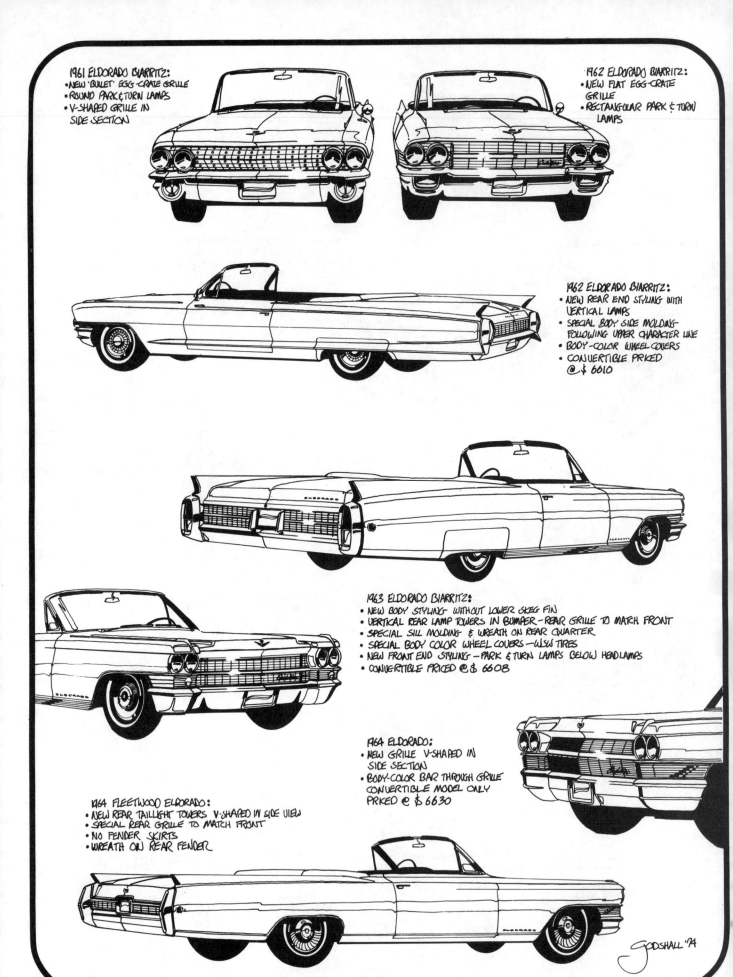

1961 ELDORADO BIARRITZ:
• NEW 'BULLET' EGG-CRATE GRILLE
• ROUND PARK & TURN LAMPS
• V-SHAPED GRILLE IN
  SIDE SECTION

1962 ELDORADO BIARRITZ:
• NEW FLAT EGG-CRATE
  GRILLE
• RECTANGULAR PARK & TURN
  LAMPS

1962 ELDORADO BIARRITZ:
• NEW REAR END STYLING WITH
  VERTICAL LAMPS
• SPECIAL BODY SIDE MOLDING
  FOLLOWING UPPER CHARACTER LINE
• BODY-COLOR WHEEL COVERS
• CONVERTIBLE PRICED
  @ $ 6610

1963 ELDORADO BIARRITZ:
• NEW BODY STYLING WITHOUT LOWER SKEG FIN
• VERTICAL REAR LAMP TOWERS IN BUMPER - REAR GRILLE TO MATCH FRONT
• SPECIAL SILL MOLDING & WREATH ON REAR QUARTER
• SPECIAL BODY COLOR WHEEL COVERS - WSW TIRES
• NEW FRONT END STYLING - PARK & TURN LAMPS BELOW HEADLAMPS
• CONVERTIBLE PRICED @ $ 6608

1964 ELDORADO:
• NEW GRILLE V-SHAPED IN
  SIDE SECTION
• BODY-COLOR BAR THROUGH GRILLE
  CONVERTIBLE MODEL ONLY
  PRICED @ $ 6630

1964 FLEETWOOD ELDORADO:
• NEW REAR TAILLIGHT TOWERS V-SHAPED IN SIDE VIEW
• SPECIAL REAR GRILLE TO MATCH FRONT
• NO FENDER SKIRTS
• WREATH ON REAR FENDER

GODSHALL '74

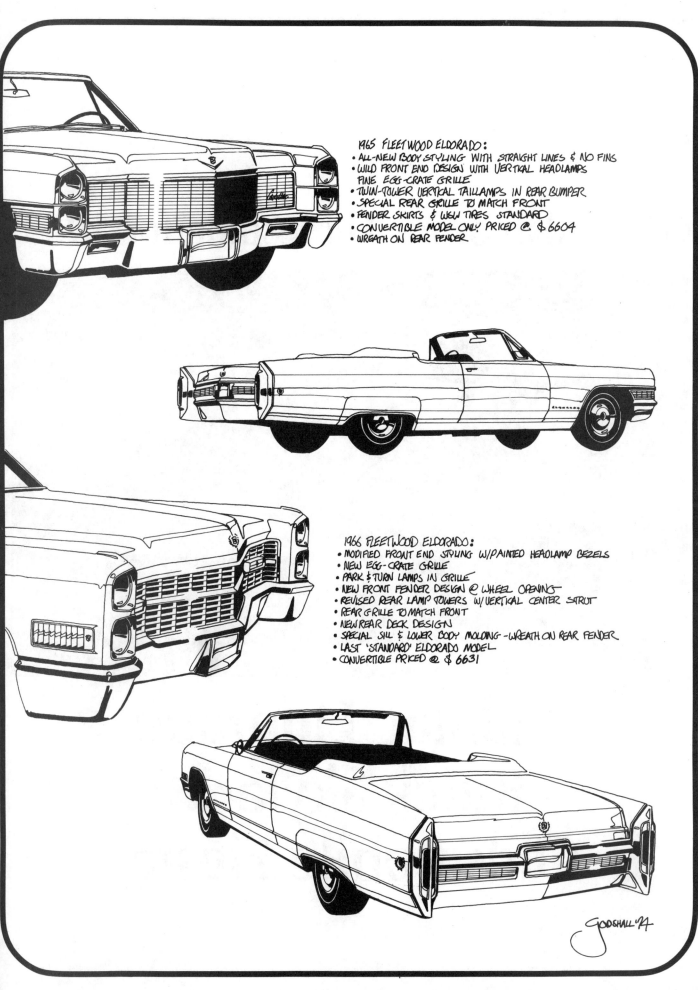

1965 FLEETWOOD ELDORADO:
- ALL-NEW BODY STYLING WITH STRAIGHT LINES & NO FINS
- WILD FRONT END DESIGN WITH VERTICAL HEADLAMPS
- FINE EGG-CRATE GRILLE
- TWIN-TOWER VERTICAL TAILLAMPS IN REAR BUMPER
- SPECIAL REAR GRILLE TO MATCH FRONT
- FENDER SKIRTS & WSW TIRES STANDARD
- CONVERTIBLE MODEL ONLY PRICED @ $6604
- WREATH ON REAR FENDER

1966 FLEETWOOD ELDORADO:
- MODIFIED FRONT END STYLING W/PAINTED HEADLAMP BEZELS
- NEW EGG-CRATE GRILLE
- PARK & TURN LAMPS IN GRILLE
- NEW FRONT FENDER DESIGN @ WHEEL OPENING
- REVISED REAR LAMP TOWERS W/VERTICAL CENTER STRUT
- REAR GRILLE TO MATCH FRONT
- NEW REAR DECK DESIGN
- SPECIAL SILL & LOWER BODY MOLDING - WREATH ON REAR FENDER
- LAST 'STANDARD' ELDORADO MODEL
- CONVERTIBLE PRICED @ $6631

GODSHALL '84

GM's Glamorous Threesome for 1953

Cadillac Eldorado
Buick Skylark
Oldsmobile Fiesta

Originally published in Special Interest Autos #134, Mar.-Apr. 1993

by John G. Tennyson
photos by the author

A NEW president, the end of the Korean War, a time of new prosperity...that was the real beginning of the "fifties era" as we know it today. 1953 was, perhaps, a turning point in the United States, not only in peacetime and politics, but for American automobiles as well.

For most of Detroit, 1953 peacetime promised to be a better but not necessarily spectacular production year. Studebaker was completely redesigned, with striking new low-slung styling. But most cars from GM, Ford, Chrysler, Packard, Nash, Hudson and Kaiser-Willys were mild face-lifts of the previous year's models, albeit more attractively styled. Longer wheelbases, more glass, chrome and heavier grilles were featured. Buick finally introduced a new ohv V-8, several years after most other competitors had already abandoned the straight eight. Twelve-volt electrics were offered on some lines in order to handle a host of expanding accessories, like power windows, seats, and air conditioning. Power steering was now standard on some luxury models. Ford, Buick and Cadillac were celebrating 50 years of production.

What makes 1953 unique in American automobile lore, however, was the willingness of some manufacturers, particularly General Motors, to make available to the public what were originally prototype show cars.

It was probably not much of a gamble. GM had used roving Motorama car shows since 1949 to both tease and test the public with new designs for possible future production. In fact, many show cars were but modifications of existing production models.

Dream cars, such as the Buick "Y Job," had been the forte of GM designers, led by Harley Earl, since the 1930s. As early as World War II, Earl reputedly sought to design his cars after fighter aircraft, notably the P-38, the genesis of Cadillac's postwar fins. That plane's bubble-top canopy was also the inspiration for panoramic windshields on GM's early fifties' show cars. Hence, in view of their own history of design, GM's move from show car to production car was entirely logical.

At the 1952 Motoramas, there was a host of dream cars, many two-seater fiberglass sports models, such as the Buick Wildcat, Cadillac LeMans and Chevrolet Corvette. But there were also the larger all-steel variations of production cars, the half-roofed Pontiac Parisienne (see *SIA* #123), as well as the Oldsmobile Fiesta, Buick Skylark, and

Cadillac Eldorado convertibles. Unlike previous Motorama show cars, the larger Olds, Buick and Cadillac models, and, of course, the Corvette, were actually brought into production. It was supposedly GM's response to the European sports cars, just starting to spark interest in the United States, but Corvette was the only one of the four which actually resembled a sports car. The other three convertibles were large, six-passenger customized luxury cars.

The ostensible occasion was the 50th Anniversary — at least for Buick and Cadillac. Olds — an older marque — joined in too. GM couldn't really expect to recoup its costs. Prices were far above those of even the highest priced standard Cadillac or Packard convertibles, aimed, perhaps, only for those of celebrity status. But like the show cars before them, GM's fabulous threesome were designed to bolster the prestige and sales of the regular lines, as well as whet the public's appetite for the future. Many of the features of the Motorama cars, the wraparound windshields, the full exposed rear wheels on Buicks, and the cut-down doors and belt-line "dip," were, indeed built into many 1954 and later GM production models.

GM's threesome chosen for this report belong to the Ramshead Collection, a private collection of two Sacramento, California, businessmen. All are white with red — and in the case of the Olds, orange-red — leather interiors.

Oldsmobile Fiesta

Of the three cars, the Olds, an older and mostly cosmetic restoration, is the rarest. The Fiesta has most of the same modifications, like the cut-down doors, of the other models. At a glance, however, except for the panoramic windshield, the Olds appears to be the least customized of the three.

The cowl had to be modified, as did the hood, to accept the new windshield. Top height was cut three inches from the Olds 98 convertible, and specially fabricated doors and a notable "dip" in the beltline, also characteristic of the Cadillac and Buick, were all part of the Fiesta's motif. The Fiesta was also fitted with special "spinner" hubcaps, which became a trademark on later Oldsmobiles and popular in the aftermarket as well.

On the outside, everything else was largely standard Olds: a huge chrome-bumper combination, with bumper guards built into the grille, a variation on other GM designs. The side treatment was massive, with rear fender skirts and upper portions of the rear

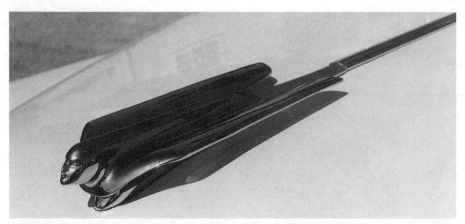

Above and below: Three distinctive hood ornaments adorn the cars: Caddy's traditional flying lady; Buick's new-for-'53 split V for its V-8; Olds's familiar rocket. Bottom: Authentic wire wheels for the Eldo and Skylark, but Fiesta makes do with spinner caps.

SIA comparisonReport

fenders and trunk painted a contrasting color and separated from the lower body by a chrome sweepspear. The Ramshead car also sports the dealer-installed continental kit with extended bumper, giving the Fiesta an even longer and more customized look. Without the continental spare, Olds rear end styling is rather plain, in contrast to the rest of the car.

Mechanically, the 98's 303-c.i.d. V-8, a bored and stroked version of the "Rocket" engine first introduced in 1949, received special manifolding with a four-barrel carburetor and an increase in compression of 8.3:1 over the standard 8:1. However, at 170 horses,

there was only a five-horsepower advantage over the Olds 98. A four-speed HydraMatic automatic transmission and a faster rear axle ratio were designed to keep the heavier 4,459 pound Fiesta within the acceptable range of expected Olds performance.

On the inside, the white leather upholstery with reddish-orange inserts is not the least subtle — looking like it might well belong in a circus. Almost every accessory available on lesser Olds models was standard on the Fiesta.

The price tag of $5,715 — some $700 more than the Skylark, and even $500 more than a Packard Caribbean convertible — was apparently just too steep for most people. After all, an Olds 98 convertible listed for only $2,963. With only 458 copies, the Fiesta convertible was dropped, and the most expensive Olds convertible for 1954 became the

Olds 98 Starfire at $3,249. But then the Starfire was not a custom-built car.

Buick Skylark

The Skylark, even without the wrap-around windshield common to the Olds and Cadillac, is perhaps the most customized looking of the three, though in reality the least. Using a Roadmaster body, the conventional windshield was lowered. The doors and mid-section were cut down like the others, but the mid-body "dip" was made to look more pronounced. What really gives the Skylark a more custom appearance, however, is the full wheel cut-out design of the rear fenders, a feature not common to the other special cars or to any other Buick at the time. The fully exposed wheels are further accentuated by an extension of the traditional Buick side body sweepspear. Instead of ending at the front of the rear wheel wells, as in previous Buicks, the sweepspear bounds up and around the wheel well and trails back to the taillamps on a horizontal plane parallel with the fender line. This styling feature was adopted on some 1954 production Buicks and lasted through 1957.

Additionally, the Kelsey-Hayes wire wheels give the Skylark a more sporty look than the Olds spinners, and the Skylark has several unique features, such as special badges ahead of the rear wheel cut-outs, a special Anniversary Edition emblem on the steering wheel hub, with a picture of a 1903 Buick and an inscription of the original owner's name, and an engine-turned appliqué on the face of the dash. The Skylark was also clean shaven, free of the traditional Buick "portholes" on the front fenders, but the Roadmaster insignias still remain on the front bumper and decklid.

New for 1953 was a Buick V-8 of 322 cubic inches, replacing the old straight eight, which Buick has used since the 1930s. The engine was one of the most efficient in the industry at the time, producing 188 horsepower with 8.5:1 compression. The smaller and lighter

engine allowed Buick to chop six inches off the length of the '53 Roadmaster, as compared with previous models. The same basic block, with periodic increases in bore and other modifications, was used through 1969.

In addition to the new V-8, Buick modified its sluggish but smooth Dynaflow automatic transmission and came up with the so-called Twin-Turbine Dynaflow, to provide a 10 percent improvement in performance.

Like Olds, the Skylark came with a host of standard features, such as power steering, brakes, front seat and windows, a special "Selectronic" radio with foot control, and electric antenna. Seating is, of course, leather, with needlepoint style red carpeting and two-toned white seats with red pleated inserts and piping on our featured car, a colorful package not unlike the Olds.

The Ramshead Buick, a mostly original car with some mechanical and cosmetic refurbishing, was purchased in 1985 sight unseen from an Ohio man, who had owned and garaged the car since 1954, and whose wife had only used it for proverbial Sunday drives. So well maintained was the Buick, it could have been driven from Ohio to California.

The Skylark, the least costly of the threesome, was still, at $5,000, more expensive than a $4,200 Cadillac 62 convertible. Some 1,690 were produced, and the Skylark was carried over for one more year, although on the shorter Special-Century chassis.

Cadillac Eldorado

The Eldorado was the most expensive American car in 1953. The custom convertible was the first of Cadillac's so-called "personal" production luxury cars. Based on the Series 62 convertible, the Eldo, like the Fiesta, came with Cadillac's first panoramic windshield, cut-down doors, and special leather interior. Colors were limited to white, ochre, red and blue.

Power steering, brakes, windows, front seat, underseat heater, signal-

All three cars are sportier than their regular production convertible counterparts, but Skylark appears to have the sportiest styling of the trio.

seeking radio, along with HydraMatic, wire wheels, a unique "Electro Vac" windshield wiper motor, which could be turned on to assist the vacuum wipers when needed, and almost every other conceivable amenity, were standard. The only accessory not available on the Eldo was air conditioning, and the price of the car was a whopping $7,750.

Unique to the Eldo, and not found on any of the other GM specialty cars, was a special metal boot cover, which fit flush with the body, giving a more streamlined appearance. The cover remains in position as a shelf when the top is up. To put down the top, a rear section, along with the small glass rear

window, can be unfastened, and the hinged metal cover unlatched and pulled through the rear opening. The top can then be lowered, using a convenient switch next to the power window button above the left rear seat armrest. When the top is down, the hatch cover is lowered and locks back into place.

Every car was virtually hand built. The hood, doors, cowl, and dash had to be modified to accommodate the special wraparound windshield. The doors and rear quarters were cut down to give a more streamlined appearance, the top about three inches lower than the standard 62 convertible, on which the Eldo

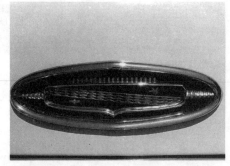
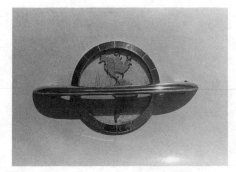

Above: All three emblems are unchanged from ordinary GM offerings. *Below:* Cad and Olds introduced wraparound windshields to the world, but Buick opted for slightly chopped stock unit. *Facing page:* How many pounds of chrome do these cars carry?

SIA comparisonReport

was based. The frame and suspension were beefed up to accept the extra weight, but the brakes and engine remained that of the regular 62 series.

The power plant, Cadillac's standard 331-c.i.d. V-8, with 210 horses, four-barrel carburetion and dual exhaust, coupled to a four-speed HydraMatic automatic transmission, made Cadillac the most powerful 1953 American car in terms of horsepower.

The Eldorado's special interiors include a padded leather dash and aluminum trim, which extend into the door panels. Front seats, custom made for the Eldo, were covered in rich pleated leather, available in solid or two-tone combinations. Some hardware, like the inside door handles, were purloined from Cadillac's limousine. Gold emblems grace the dash and door sills.

The '53 was the first in a long line of Eldorados, but few would match the custom-built character of the original.

Our featured Eldorado is a fairly new ground-up restoration of a nice original car and, with less than 500 miles on the odometer, drives and handles like brand new.

Similarities and Differences

The three GM Motorama production cars had much in common. They were all lowered convertibles, based on the top-of-the-line model, with cut-down doors, a full array of power accessories as standard equipment, special leather interiors and various custom touches, like special emblems and special wheels, to name a few.

But the three cars were also quite distinctive, while maintaining their badge identities with standard models. The Olds and Cadillac had the new panoramic windshield, the Buick a conventional, though chopped windscreen. The Buick had full rear wheel cut-outs, while the Olds and Cadillac were skirted. The Olds had the only engine modified from the standard line — though only by five horses. The Cadillac was much heavier and somewhat larger

Comparison of Major Styling Features

Feature	Eldorado	Skylark	Fiesta
Windshield	Panoramic	Conventional but chopped	Panoramic
Vent windows	Frameless	Conventional	Frameless
Doors	Cut down	Cut down	Cut down
Quarters	Beltline "dip"	Beltline "dip"	Beltline "dip"
Distinguishing side treatment	Rear fender scoop	Full body sweepspear	Rear fender sweepspear
Rear fender	Skirted wheels	Exposed wheels	Skirted wheels
Wheels	Wire	Wire	Conventional spinner caps
Body color	Solid	Solid	Rear two-tone
Hood ornament	Flying goddess	Bombsight	Rocket ship
Boot cover	Hinged, flush-fitted metal	Snap-on conventional	Snap-on conventional

than the Buick and Olds, the Buick the smallest and lightest of the three, though none of these cars was small by any means.

The Buick is thought by many to be the most attractive, and truest to the concept of the "sporty" car, which these limited-production convertibles were said to represent. This is no doubt due to the unique rear fenders and more pronounced beltline "dip." But the Buick is somewhat shorter than the others, and thus the interior seating position, particularly leg room for tall drivers, and head room with the top up, is more cramped. The Olds and Cadillac, while streamlined, seem somehow more massive and chrome-laden than the Buick. But then, the Buick does not feature the more dramatic panoramic windshield, frameless vent windows, or reworked cowl and custom padded dash of the others, nor does Buick's revised Dynaflow transmission compare as favorably to the performance offered by the Olds and Cadillac HydraMatic.

Of the three in the Ramshead Collection, the Cadillac is the best driver, probably because of its recent and extensive restoration. It's also the most luxurious and impressive of the three GM specialty convertibles, as well as more attractive than bulkier looking Eldorados of the mid and late fifties. The wraparound windshield and lowered doors give the Cadillac a sporty flair without altering the Cadillac "style." The metal boot cover provides a custom look, and the rich dash, gold emblems, and semi-bucket seats done in leather provide the luxury touch. Again, the Skylark appears to be the most distinctive, in comparison to standard Buicks, while the Fiesta, on the outside, seems the least changed from its basic Olds 98 counterpart.

1953 Comparison Specifications

	Cadillac Eldorado	Buick Skylark	Oldsmobile Fiesta
Price (f.o.b.	$7,750	$5,000	$5,715
Body style	2-dr, 6-pass. convert.	2-dr, 6-pass. convert.	2-dr, 6-pass. convert.
Chassis	Ladder frame, Central X member	Ladder frame Central X member	Ladder frame Central X member
Wheelbase	126.0 inches	121.5 inches	124.0 inches
Length	220.8 inches	207.6 inches	215.0 inches
Width	80.1 inches	79.9 inches	76.9 inches
Height	58.5 inches	N/A	N/A
Front track	59.1 inches	60.0 inches	59.0 inches
Rear track	63.1 inches	62.0 inches	59.0 inches
Weight	4,800 lb. (cw)	4,315 lb. (cw)	4,459 lb. (sw)
Engine	ohv V-8	ohv V-8	ohv V-8
Displacement	331 c.i.d.	322 c.i.d.	303 c.i.d.
Bore/stroke	3.813 x 3.625 inches	4.00 x 3.20 inches	3.75 x 3.44 inches
Compress.	8.25:1	8.5:1	8.3:1
Horsepower	210 @ 4,150 rpm	188 @ 4,000 rpm	170 @ 3,600 rpm
Torque	330 lb/ft @ 2,700 rpm	N/A	284 @ 1,800 rpm
Carb	4-bbl	4-bbl	4-bbl
Exhaust	Dual	Single	Single
Transmission	HydraMatic 4-speed	Dynaflow 2-speed	HydraMatic 4-speed
Rear axle	Hypoid	Hypoid	Hypoid
Ratio	3.77:1	N/A	3.42:1
Suspension	Front, independent, coil springs; rear, solid axle, leaf springs	Front, independent, coil springs; rear, solid axle, leaf springs	Front, independent, coil springs; rear, solid axle, leaf springs
Brakes	Hydraulic, power 4-wheel drum	Hydraulic, power 4-wheel drum	Hydraulic, power 4-wheel drum
Drums	12 inch	N/A	11 inch
Swept area	258 sq. in.	N/A	191.7 sq. in.
Steering	Recirculating ball power assist	Recirculating ball power assist	Recirculating ball power assist
Lock/lock	5 turns	N/A	5.5 turns
Tires	8.00x15 inches	8.00x15 inches	8.00x15 inches
# produced	532	1,690	458

SIA comparisonReport

Cadillac rear styling is quite graceful; Buick's sleek and modern for '53; Olds makes long even longer with accessory continental kit.

Where are they now?

The threesome — The Eldorado, Skylark, and Fiesta — were a bold move, but then the Chrysler Town and Country woodie sedans, convertibles and hardtops, and Continental Mark II are also evidence that manufacturers were, perhaps, more willing to take chances with limited production specialty cars in those days. None of them lasted as semi-customs, and their names were later hijacked for other, and often rather mundane, production cars.

In the case of Olds, the Fiesta was dropped after only one year. The name later appeared on 1957-58 Oldsmobile station wagon offerings. The Skylark was continued through 1954 but on a smaller Special-Century chassis and, with even more dismal production (836) than in 1953, was not offered for 1955. The Skylark name was revived in 1961 as a sporty and more luxurious version of Buick's compact Special, and the Skylark continues today as Buick's compact two- and four-door model.

Through the years, the Eldorado has had a more successful career as a luxury line. In fact, until the Seville, the Eldo was the top-of-the-line Cadillac for more than 20 years. It was a dressed-up production line 62 convertible in 1954, with a strip of stainless metal on the lower rear fenders, and the price was dropped by $2,000. In 1955, unique shark-like fins set the Eldo

Above: Metal boot gives Eldo very smooth, sleek appearance. Other cars use conventional vinyl covers. **Below:** Buick's open wheel treatment looks more rakish than skirted rivals.

Above: All dashes display an abundance of chrome. *Below:* And all three are motivated by V-8s ranging from 170 to 210 bhp.

SIA comparisonReport

apart from other Cadillacs. The Eldorado convertible became the Eldorado Biarritz in 1956, and a two-door hardtop Eldorado Seville was added to the line. An ultra-expensive custom Eldorado Brougham four-door was offered from '57 through '60 on a very limited basis. Eldorado convertibles were continued through 1966, but Eldorados in the sixties were almost indistinguishable from the standard Cadillac line. An all new "personal" front-wheel-drive two-door hardtop Eldorado was introduced in 1967, and the Eldorado convertible was re-introduced in 1971 and lasted through 1976. The first downsized 1979-1985 Eldorados were also attractive, and a limited number of reworked hardtops appeared as convertibles in the last few model years. After 1985, the Eldorado became a cookie-cutter compact with a luxury price, barely recognizable as a Cadillac. The 1992 and later models show more promise of reviving the standard.

The fabulous threesome from GM are truly unique, not only as one-year models, but in the fact they represent a special effort by one manufacturer to bring three separate customized cars to the market simultaneously — the kind of expensive effort that we shall probably not see repeated in our lifetimes. ❑

*All three trunks are nicely finished, but Eldo's, **above,** has a nearly custom-tailored appearance.*

CADILLAC LOST an estimated $10,000 every time a dealer sold a new Eldorado Brougham. Lincoln fared a little better—they lost only about $1000 on each Mark II Continental.

So is it safe to say that both cars ended up magnificent failures? From a cost accountant's viewpoint, yes. From an auto enthusiast's, definitely not.

If you get a chance to examine a 1956-7 Mark II or a 1957-8 Brougham closely, do. Check beneath the doors or the way the hood braces are painted, or run your finger along the lip behind a bumper pan. You'll find them finished with much more care than the exposed surfaces of ordinary cars.

Most people didn't realize it then, nor do they now, but General Motors and Ford were waging a quiet war with these two super-luxury cars. It wasn't the hoot-and-holler sort we're used to among the lower-priced makes—it was very subdued, polite, proper, non-violent, and deadly serious. The Continental came out first, and if it hadn't been for the Mark II, there would have been no Brougham. Both ended up as drastic mistakes. Both companies lost money and to some extent lost face. The market pulse-takers at Ford and GM misjudged the salability of big cars in the late 1950s and didn't expect an economic recession. By 1958, the fickle U.S. car-buying public would swing away from the higher-priced makes and slide into compacts and economy imports.

ever since they'd dropped the "Mark I" in 1948, Lincoln dealers kept asking Ford Motor Co. for a new Continental. Dearborn stalled but finally decided to find out whether a revival would sell.

In early 1952, Ford ordered some Edsel-style market research. It was a tough topic to spell out—no one knew exactly what kind of car the researchers were talking about (including the researchers). According to FORTUNE in an article published at the Mark II's introduction in 1955: "Continental's own delvings into individual net worth, disposable income, multiple-car ownership, private school registration, and the like have led it to conclude that there are 250,000 to 300,000 families in the U.S. that could afford such a purchase....On the other hand, the thinness of the market for a $10,000 automobile may have already been intimated by U.S. sales of similarly priced foreign makes—less than 200 a year."

The Mark II was going to be a gamble, no doubt about that. At stake was that indefinable "Gold Standard" among American luxury cars, a standard held for decades by Cadillac. If Lincoln were ever to capture the Gold Standard, it would have to be with something so sumptuous, so luxurious, so fine (and all those other superlatives) that it would immediately

Mark II Me

make a prestige car buyer react, "Ah! Lincoln Continental," instead of an automatic, "Ah! Cadillac!"

Ford's researchers—the Davis Committee—recommended to management to go ahead with the Mark II even if it meant losing money. Their report concluded: "Even though not directly justifiable on a financial basis, the institutional advertising value of the Continental... warrants adaptation of the program." In other words, even at a loss, the Mark II would pay its way in publicity and prestige.

Cadillac later said nearly the same thing. "We'll lose our shirt on every one [Brougham] that leaves the plant," confided a Cad exec to a FORTUNE reporter. In 1956, James M. Roche, then Cadillac's general sales manager, confirmed that (to quote AUTOMOTIVE INDUSTRIES), "Cadillac does not expect to make real money on the new Brougham...." Thus the battle for the automotive Gold Standard was on, and no one cared much about the expense.

Coming up with a ready-made classic happens to be a very difficult assignment. You don't just *do* it. FoMoCo management handed the project to William Clay (Bill) Ford, then 26. Bill chose six men, all young, and set up a makeshift studio in the old Henry Ford Trade School. He'd been given 10 months and $1 million to come up with "the picture." His key men were stylist John Reinhart, who'd worked with Gordon Buehrig on the coffin-nosed Cord, and Harley Copp, chief engineer of Ford's Special Product Operation. Buehrig himself was later called in to do some of the body engineering.

In the Davis Committee's original recommendations, the Mark II's price was set at no more than $8000 retail and its design was to be "good for at least four years without major change." What the researchers couldn't spell out was what the Continental should look like. Bill Ford and John Reinhart worked very hard to make the car look traditional and classic, yet at the same time to incorporate what they called Modern Formal. By the end of 1952, Bill thought they had it. He called a special meeting of all major Ford men. "The picture" stood behind velvet curtains. When these parted, dead silence. Henry Ford II finally broke it with, "I wouldn't give you a dime for that."

The Trade School boys were, of course, crushed, but all of them went back to work the next day. After long discussion, they decided to keep the same basic outline but to refine the details. At the same time they bought some insurance by calling in four outside designers to submit independent concepts. Finally, in April, 1953, Bill Ford again called an executive meeting.

This time all five designs hung side by side in a bare room. Each viewer was ushered in one at a time so no one could wink, nod, or signal anyone else. Each in turn picked Reinhart's design.

From that point on, it became a matter of working out the details, although that makes it sound a lot easier than it was. Harley Copp had a few rough moments designing a frame low enough to accomodate the 56-inch body height and yet strong enough to carry 5000-plus pounds. He solved both problems with square-tube crossmembers and by running the exhaust pipes inside the frame rails.

During the Mark II's early stages, the Trade School group hoped to include a convertible and perhaps a 4-door sedan in the line. They seriously considered the retractable hardtop that Ford later introduced on the 1957 Skyliner. They also experimented with fuel injection for the 368-cid Lincoln V-8, getting fantastic power increases with it. But production costs were mounting, and the Mark II's base price was already over $8000, so the retractable roof, the extra body styles, and fuel injection went by the board.

Ford Motor Co. set up a separate Continental Div., distinct and apart from Lincoln-Mercury Div. They built a special $25 million plant near Dearborn for the Mark II's production. As introduction drew near, rumors leaked that potential owners would be checked for social standing, and a number of pre-production orders came in accompanied by pages from the *Social Register*. TIME Magazine reported (incorrectly) that 2100 orders had been placed by the eve of introduction and that Argentine ex-dictator Juan Peron's was among them.

To break even, Continental Div. had to sell a minimum of 2500 Mark II's per year for a 4-year cycle. As it turned out, they sold 4660 in two years and then stopped building the Mark II body style altogether. This resulted in an estimated loss of approximately $1000 per unit.

When General Motors got wind of Ford's plan to dethrone Cadillac with the Mark II, they considered the threat serious enough to retaliate.

Throughout the 1950s, GM held what they called "Motoramas." These were elaborate shows staged in major cities each year. They featured the new season's production models plus a number of experimentals and show cars to test public reaction and add spice. More spice came by way of pretty girls, music, and usually a stage revue.

The Cadillac Eldorado Brougham had its ancestors in these Motorama shows. The design itself evolved from the 1953 Cadillac Orleans and the Cadillac Park Avenue of 1954. The Orleans was the industry's first genuine 4-door hardtop, and the Park Avenue followed with a brushed aluminum roof.

The Brougham was basically the brainchild of Harley Earl, GM's strong-minded vice presi-

s Eldorado Brougham

Eldorado Brougham Chronology

May 1954: GM execs meet to discuss Eldorado Brougham project. Cadillac styling studio given go-ahead to do clays. So far Brougham planned only as 1-off show car to test public reaction.

Aug. 1954: Clay models completed, previewed by top management.

Nov. 1954: Cadillac Div. delivers special show car chassis and under-body to Styling.

Jan. 19, 1954: Brougham show car's first public display at GM Motorama, NYC. Reaction highly favorable.

Mar. 1955: GM Motorama, San Francisco, Cad announces plans for limited production of Eldorado Brougham during 1956, begins engineering and styling production prototype.

Dec. 1955: Production proto shown for 1st time at 42nd Paris Auto Show.

Jan. 19, 1956: GM Motorama, NYC, production proto first shown in U.S. Cadillac announces price at "about $8500," projects production at 1500 per year.

Feb. - Jun. 1956: Three test cars built and tested at GM's Desert Proving Grounds, Mesa, Ariz.

Jul. - Nov. 1956: Even more innovations planned and tested than reach production, e.g. fuel injection, Hydra-Matic transaxle, wet disc brakes, 4-wheel independent suspension.

Dec. 8, 1956: N.Y. Auto Show, first public display of production Eldorado Brougham.

Mar. 18, 1957: First shipment of Broughams goes to selected dealers. New list price: $13,074 f.o.b.

Jul. 1958: Eldorado Brougham production ceases, 704 built in all. Outside estimates put factory costs at $23,000 per car, a loss to Cadillac of nearly $10,000 each.

Continental Mark II Chronology

Early 1952: Ford Motor Co. decides to explore ways to revive classic Lincoln Continental, discontinued since 1948 (5322 "Mark I's" built between 1939-48). Reason for discussions: Dealers clamor for new prestige car.

Jun. 1952: Davis Committee draws up secret preliminary cost and price analyses, projects Mark II's tag at $8000 and break-even at 2500 cars a year.

Aug. 1952: Wm. Clay Ford, stylist John Reinhart, and engineer Harley Copp given charge of design, $1 million and 10 months to come up with "the picture."

Dec. 1952: Design group unveils first styling drawings to assembled FoMoCo execs. Execs thumbs it down.

Apr. 1953: Design group holds 2nd styling showing. Five alternatives given—4 outside and 1 company. Execs choose company design.

Late 1953: Ford engineers begin experiments to incorporate retractable hardtop and fuel injection in Mark II. Both tried but rejected as too costly.

Early 1954: Copp successfully demonstrates that cowbelly frame with square-tube crossmembers will hold Continental's weight, achieves hoped-for lowness.

Most of 1955: Prototypes tested, production facilities set up. Projected list price raised to $10,000. Continental Div. becomes formal, separate entity.

Oct. 21, 1955: Continental Mark II unveiled publicly for 1st time. *TIME* Magazine reports that 2100 orders have already come in.

Aug. 1957: Production of Mark II ceases. Total built: 4660.

(Top left) 1953 Cadillac Orleans show car was first 4-door hardtop, influenced Eldo, as did 1954 Park Avenue (top right). By '56, Cadillac planned but never built Eldo towncar. Derham, tho, made 2 Mark II converts.

Eldo Meets Mark II

What do you get for $13,074?

Following is a list of standard equipment on the 1957-58 Cadillac Eldorado Brougham.

- Air conditioning.
- Individual front & rear heating systems with underseat blowers.
- 6-way power front seat with twin "Favorite Position" memory settings.
- Power steering, brakes, windows (including ventipanes).
- Automatic power door locks.
- Electric trunk lid with dashboard control (raises and lowers lid electrically).
- Fully carpeted trunk.
- Air suspension with automatic load leveling. Rubber airbags take the place of conventional metal springs.
- Hydra-Matic automatic transmission.
- Automatic headlight dimmer.
- Lamps: quad headlights, fog, backup, all compartments.
- Glovebox vanity with 6 silver magnetized tumblers, fold-out shelf/mirror, cigarette case, tissue dispenser, lipstick and stick cologne.
- Electric clock with drum dial.
- Cigarette lighters, 2 front, 2 rear.
- Full instrumentation plus warning lights.
- All-transistor AM radio with automatic disappearing antenna, front & rear speakers.
- Automatic engine starting and restarting.
- Polarized sunvisors that become darker by tilting.
- Grey-tinted glass in all windows.
- Armrests front & rear. Rear armrest has storage bin with notepad, pencil, mirror, perfume atomizer, Arpege.
- Choice of 45 interior trim & color choices, lambskin or Karakul carpeting.
- Forged aluminum-center wheels.
- Premium wide-oval, narrow-whitewall tires.
- Brushed stainless steel roof.
- Rubber bumper inserts.
- Quadruple horns.

What do you get for $9517?

Following is a list of standard equipment on the 1956-57 Lincoln Continental Mark II.

- Turbo-Drive automatic transmission.
- Power 4-way front seat.
- Power steering, brakes, windows.
- Dual heating system.
- Premium AM radio.
- Choice of leather, nylon broadcloth, or matelasse interiors plus deep-pile carpeting.
- Individual roof registers for optional air conditioning.
- Full instrumentation, including tachometer.
- Self-regulating electric clock that adjusts its rate automatically when hands are reset.
- Tinted glass in all windows.
- Rear armrest.
- Turbo-finned wheel covers.
- Premium whitewall tires.
- Fully carpeted trunk.
- Twin exhausts.
- Engine dress-up kit.

Brougham's doors automatically lock in 14-inch posts when shut. Car has no central body pillars.

Brougham carries much more brightwork than Mark II, and Eldo shop manual devotes 6 pages to refurbishing stainless steel roof, which scratches easily. Both cars move out quickly, in great silence.

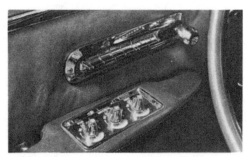

Not visible here: Eldo's sunvisors are polarized plastic, become darker the steeper their angle.

Tumblers stand atop compartment inside glovebox door. Beneath are cosmetics, cigs, tissues.

Door controls include 6-way "memory" power seat, buttons for door locks, electric windows.

Conti's dash is much simpler than Eldo's, in fact seems spartan, yet includes all gauges and tach.

Mark II has 4 roof registers for air conditioning. Passengers tend to complain of cold heads.

Fair leg room in rear seat makes this strictly a 4-seat coupe. Door pillars have chromed plates.

Brougham's trunklid raises and lowers with electric motor, is activated by button in glovebox or key. If battery goes dead, no access to trunk.

Mark II's trunk is blocked by spare, which also cuts severely into space. Perhaps if tire cantilevered backwards like Zephyr's, it'd be handier.

1956 Lincoln Continental Mark II coupe

Price when new . . . . $9517 f.o.b. Dearborn (1956).
Current valuation . . . . Xlnt. $4540; gd. $2940. *

ENGINE
Type . . . . Ohv V-8, water-cooled, cast-iron block.
Bore & stroke . . . . 4.00 x 3.66 in.
Displacement . . . . 368 cu. in.
Max. bhp @ rpm . . . . . 285 @ 4000 (In 1957, 300 @ 4800).
Max. torque @ rpm . . . . 402 @ 3000 (In 1957, 415 @ 3000).
Compression ratio . . . . . 9.0:1 (In 1957, 10.0:1).
Induction system . . . . . . Carter 4-bbl. carburetor.
Exhaust system . . . . Cast-iron manifolds, twin exhausts, 2 mufflers, 2 resonators.
Electrical system . . . . . . 12-volt battery/coil.

CLUTCH
Type . . . . None.

TRANSMISSION
Type . . . . Turbo-Drive 3-speed automatic, torque converter with planetary gearsets.
Ratios: 1st . . . . 2.40:1.
     2nd . . . . 1.47:1.
     3rd . . . . 1.00:1.
     Reverse . . . . 2.00:1.

DIFFERENTIAL
Type . . . . Hypoid, spiral bevel gears.
Ratio . . . . 3.07:1.
Drive axles . . . . Semi-floating.

STEERING
Type . . . . Linkage power steering (Saginaw).
Ratio . . . . 22.1:1.
Turns lock to lock . . . . . . 4.
Turn circle . . . . 45.3 ft.

BRAKES
Type . . . . 4-wheel drums, hydraulic, power assist, internal expanding.
Drum diameter . . . . 12.0 in.
Total swept area . . . . . . 207.7 sq. in.

CHASSIS & BODY
Frame . . . . Square-tube steel, double dropped.
Body . . . . All steel, 2-dr., 5-pass. coupe.
Front suspension . . . . . . Independent, unequal A-arms, coil springs, ball-joint spindles, tubular hydraulic shocks, link stabilizer bar.
Rear suspension . . . . Solid axle, longitudinal semi-elliptic springs, tubular hydraulic shocks.
Tires . . . . 8.00 x 15 tubeless whitewalls, 4-ply.
Wheels . . . . Pressed steel bolt-ons.

WEIGHTS & MEASURES
Wheelbase . . . . 126.0 in.
Front & rear tread . . . . . 58.6/60.0 in.
Overall length . . . . 218.4 in.
Overall height . . . . 56.25 in.
Overall width . . . . 77.5 in.
Ground clearance . . . . . . 6.0 in.
Curb weight . . . . 4825 lb.

CAPACITIES
Crankcase . . . . 5 qt.
Cooling system . . . . 25.5 qt.
Gas tank . . . . 25 gal.

* Courtesy **Antique Automobile Appraisal.**

1958 Cadillac Eldorado Brougham 4-dr. hardtop sedan

Price when new . . . . $13,074 f.o.b. Detroit (1958).

Current valuation . . . . Xlnt. $3900; gd. $2290. *

ENGINE
Type . . . . Ohv V-8, water-cooled, cast-iron block.
Bore & stroke . . . . 4.00 x 3.63 in.
Displacement . . . . 365 cu. in.
Max. bhp @ rpm . . . . . . 335 @ 4800.
Max. torque @ rpm . . . . 405 @ 3400.
Compression ratio . . . . . 10.25:1.
Induction system . . . . . . 3 Rochester 2-bbl. carbs, electric fuel pump suspended inside tank.
Exhaust system . . . . Cast-iron manifolds, twin exhausts, 2 mufflers, 2 resonators.
Electrical system . . . . . . 12-volt battery/coil.

CLUTCH
Type . . . . None.

TRANSMISSION
Type . . . . Hydra-Matic 4-speed automatic, torque converter with planetary gearsets.
Ratios: 1st . . . . 3.97:1.
     2nd . . . . 2.55:1.
     3rd . . . . 1.55:1.
     4th . . . . 1.00:1.
     Reverse . . . . 3.74:1.

DIFFERENTIAL
Type . . . . Hypoid, spiral-bevel gears.
Ratio . . . . 3.36:1.
Drive axles . . . . Semi-floating.

STEERING
Type . . . . Linkage power steering (Saginaw).
Ratio . . . . 19.5:1.
Turns lock to lock . . . . . . 4.25.
Turn circle . . . . 53.0 ft.

BRAKES
Type . . . . 4-wheel drums, hydraulic, power assist, internal expanding.
Drum diameter . . . . 12 in.
Total swept area . . . . . . 210.3 sq. in.

CHASSIS & BODY
Frame . . . . Central X-member.
Body . . . . All steel, 4-dr., 5-pass. hardtop sedan.
Front suspension . . . . . . Unequal A-arms, self-leveling airbags, tubular hydraulic shocks.
Rear suspension . . . . Lower trailing control links, upper single control yoke, self-leveling airbags, tubular hydraulic shocks.
Tires . . . . 8.40 x 15, 4-ply, narrow-rib whitewalls.
Wheels . . . . Cast-aluminum centers, steel rims, bolt-ons.

WEIGHTS & MEASURES
Wheelbase . . . . 126.0 in.
Front & rear tread . . . . . 61.0 in.
Overall length . . . . 216.3 in.
Overall height . . . . 55.5 in.
Overall width . . . . 78.5 in.
Ground clearance . . . . . . 5.3 to 6.3 in.
Curb weight . . . . 5420 lb.

CAPACITIES
Crankcase . . . . 6 qt.
Cooling system . . . . 22.6 qt.
Gas tank . . . . 20 gal.

PERFORMANCE (speedometer and stopwatch)
0-30 mph . . . . 4.9 sec.
0-45 mph . . . . 7.3 sec.
0-60 mph . . . . 12.9 sec.
Standing ¼ mile . . . . . . 20.0 sec. & 76.0 mph.
Top speed (est.) . . . . 110-115 mph.

FUEL CONSUMPTION
All around average . . . . . 12.07 mpg.

* Courtesy **Antique Automobile Appraisal.**

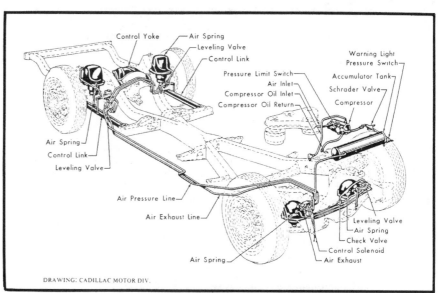

Mark II wheel cover (left) has 40 vanes, cost $26 new, now costs several times that. Eldorado wheel has cast aluminum center, steel rim.

Eldorado Brougham's suspension system consists of 4 rubber airbags, one at each wheel. Electric motor runs compressor to keep accumulator at 100-120 psi. System includes 3 leveling valves that hold constant axle clearance. We felt Brougham's ride, handling didn't match system's complexity.

Mark II uses stock 368-cid Lincoln V-8 with selected parts to assure balance, long life. Die-cast rocker covers are part of engine dress-up kit.

1957 Eldo had two 4-barrels but changed to three 2s in '58. Otherwise, Cad V-8 was stock. Eldo and Mark II were both slated for fuel injection.

Eldo Meets Mark II

dent of styling. In early 1954, Earl approached Cadillac general manager Don Ahrens with plans for the Brougham and talked about limited production. According to Dan Adams, now Cadillac's assistant chief engineer, Cad engineers went twice to GM Styling to inspect models of the proposed Brougham. Both times they decided that the cost would be prohibitive. But Management, seeing a Mark II coming down the road, over-ruled Engineering and gave a tentative go-ahead.

The Brougham's philosophy—the original thinking behind it—was entirely unlike the Mark II's. Cadillac show cars began as testbeds for scores of major and minor innovations: mechanical, technical, manufacturing, and styling. A surprising number found their way

into production. The Brougham's pillar-less 4-door hardtop body, the air suspension, forged aluminum wheels, "memory" power seat, and dozens of other gadgets came directly from Motorama showsters and experimentals.

John Mooar, a Brougham owner in Pasadena, Calif., sat down one day and counted the electric motors, relays, switches, solenoids, and light bulbs in his 1957 Eldo. The total exceeded 163. This gives some idea of how complicated the car is. Mooar, who's owned his Brougham for five years and loves it dearly, says, "As far as practicality goes, it's a nightmare." Don Pabst, president of the Cadillac agency in Santa Clara, Calif., and owner of the Brougham used for this driveReport, says that only a dealer can keep one in proper working order.

Like the creators of the Mark II, Cadillac's engineers planned even more for the Brougham than it eventually got. They, too, toyed with

fuel injection, but at the last minute stuck two 4-barrel carbs on the standard Cad V-8 instead (changed to three 2-barrels for 1958). They considered mounting the Hydra-Matic in the rear a la early Tempest, necessitating 4-wheel independent suspension. They played with wet disc brakes (running in oil) plus several less dramatic things, but none of these saw light. As it was, the Brougham turned out dramatic enough without them (see list of standard equipment).

Cadillac management did hope to introduce the Brougham earlier than they did. Continental had more than a year's jump. The first Brougham production model was shown on Dec. 8, 1956, but salable cars weren't in dealers' hands until March. Yet the delay did help GM in one way: It showed them they'd miscalculated. By the time the Brougham bowed, GM could see

Eldo Meets Mark II

the Mark II wasn't selling nearly so well as expected. At $3500 more, Cadillac saw the Eldo wouldn't either. Thus they could save some embarrassment by not pushing the Brougham too hard, and as it developed, it received a lot less publicity than the Mark II.

That was one of the blows to the Eldorado's success, but there were more. Among them: 1) The name Eldorado had been diluted by earlier Eldorados, including the 1957 Eldorado Biarritz convertible and the Eldorado Seville 2-door hardtop, each selling for a paltry $6648. 2) Cadillac's stylists had given much of the Brougham's flavor to the mainline of 1957 Cads. So the Brougham's appearance had less impact than it might have, and the car looked less distinctive on the street.

As it turned out, 704 Broughams were sold in all, 400 in 1957 and 304 in 1958. The only significant change between these was carburetion—two 4s to three 2s. Like the watered-down Mark III Continental of 1958, the Brougham name was carried over into 1959 and 1960, but these later series were hardly in the same league. They used the standard chassis and drivetrain and were fitted with bodies built in Italy. This was done mostly to reduce tooling and labor costs. In 1959, 99 Eldorado Broughams were produced, in 1960 101, but these definitely didn't show the quality and workmanship of the 1957-8 Fleetwood bodies.

In driving these two cars, we especially looked forward to the "cloud-soft" ride of the air-suspended Brougham. The ads and sales literature led us to hope for some exquisitely smooth, silent treat that combined flatiron cornering with a pillowy ride over a plowed field. But it wasn't quite like that.

Most Broughams have been converted to standard coil springs, a job that costs between $300 and $500. After much phoning and searching, we found a Brougham that still had the airbags and very low mileage (33,660), which we figured would make the car as much like new as possible. But we have to admit a certain disappointment—the ride felt no different from a conventionally suspended new Ford or Chevrolet, and the Brougham's cornering and general road feel seemed quite a bit worse. The body rolls generously, and while we didn't corner fast, we were disappointed even at low speeds.

Aside from the myriad technical innovations carried through in the Brougham, its most noteworthy feature still remains the air suspension. This consists of four rubber airdomes that take the place of metal springs, one per wheel. A small air compressor, powered by its own electric motor, feeds air to the domes via an accumulator tank whose pressure is kept at 100-120 psi. The system also includes three levelers, one up front and two in back, to keep body height even no matter what the load and also to maintain constant axle clearance. These levelers make for an eerie sensation when you sit down in the driver's seat. Suddenly the car begins to moan quietly and to gently lift you up half an inch or so.

Air suspension wasn't new with the Brougham—patents date back to 1847, when it was used on wagons. By 1958, air suspension was available optionally on all GM cars, some Fords, and as boosters on Chrysler Corp. offerings. Units at that time were made by Goodyear, Firestone, and General Tire. Greyhound buses

and some GMC and Kenworth trucks still ride on air.

The main problem with air springs is that the domes eventually either blow out or develop slow leaks. When one blows, the car falls directly on its axles ("down dead," as one Brougham owner puts it). The obvious remedy is to replace the blown airdome—it can't be patched or vulcanized. But airdomes are no longer available through GM or the manufacturer, so unless you find one in a dealer's stock or a used one in a junkyard, you're forced to go to metal springs.

If the airdome merely leaks, it means that within a few hours or a couple of days, the system loses enough pressure so the car falls down dead again. Switching on the compressor re-establishes the air supply, but it's awkward to hop into a car whose body is resting on the street and sit there until it resurrects itself. At any rate, air suspension proved one of the Brougham's weakest points—one of several, the "several" being that the reliability of any mechanism decreases in a mathematical inverse to its complexity. And the Brougham was (and is) a highly complex machine.

By way of contrast, the Continental Mark II wasn't nearly so gadget-laden. The emphasis was on quality and what Bill Ford judged to be good taste. The 1956 Mark II we drove belonged to Bob Pittman of Saratoga, Calif., a manufacturer's representative in transportation products. His car had seen over 168,000 miles, yet it felt as tight as any new one—no rattles, no noises, everything solid and in working order. Pittman bought his Continental in 1962 at 73,000 miles and still drives it nearly every day. He's had the engine overhauled twice, wrecked and repaired the front end once, and though we couldn't tell it, he felt the interior needed reupholstering.

The contrast between these two particular cars was interesting because the Brougham was nearly new while the Mark II would have to be judged "old" by any normal standard. Yet neither of these *is* a normal car. During assembly, parts were especially chosen for near-perfect tolerances. Cadillac coded these parts "CD," and Continental Div. had a similar designation. Assembly time for the Brougham was 13 days whereas the Mark II was built with four times the labor content as a regular 1956 Lincoln and eight times as much as a Ford. The Mark II engine was basically Lincoln but was put through six hours of dyno testing before installation. Continentals were shipped to dealers in special fleece-lined plastic-with-canvas envelopes.

These two cars possibly mark the finest flowering of semi-mass-produced American automobiles. Major automakers will likely never try anything like them again, and the independents who've tried cars like these (the revived Duesenberg and now Stutz) apparently face even greater odds than did GM and Ford.

The current front-drive Eldorado lists for $6903, while the confusingly designated new Mark III carries a base price of $7281. But nowadays it's just inflation—it's no longer a battle for the Gold Standard. □

The editors thank car owners Bob Pittman, Saratoga, Calif. (Mark II) and Don Pabst, Pres., St. Claire Cadillac, Santa Clara, Calif.; Cyrus W. Strickler, III, Atlanta, Ga., and John Mooar, Pasadena, Calif., for technical assistance; the Lincoln Continental Owners Club, Post Office Box 549, Nogales, Ariz. 85621; Lincoln-Mercury Div. of Ford Motor Co.; and Cadillac Div. of General Motors.

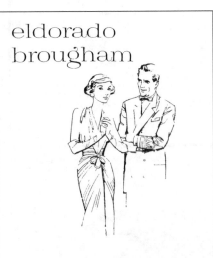

eldorado brougham

Because of its exclusive, custom-built character, the Eldorado Brougham for 1958 will continue to be built in limited numbers. This dramatically beautiful car—with its brushed stainless steel roof . . . air suspension . . . special engine . . . and many other revolutionary new engineering developments—has been created to be the finest motor car of all time. Cadillac permits no compromise in styling . . . design . . . engineering . . . or in excellence of craftsmanship. Only by making a personal inspection of this car will you understand how markedly advanced the Eldorado Brougham actually is in styling . . . in luxury . . . and in performance.

The custom-crafted interiors of the Eldorado Brougham are exclusively fashioned in the world's finest leathers and fabrics. In all, there are forty-four selections of trims and colors. Carpeting is either nylon Karakul or genuine mouton. The rear armrest is fitted with a vanity mirror and perfume atomizer containing Arpège Extrait de Lanvin.

There is a difference, too, that can't be seen

Continental
Mark II

Continental Division · Ford Motor Company

SIA comparisonReport

1961 Cadillac, Imperial and Lincoln

by John G. Tennyson
photos by the author

BY most standards, 1961 was an American milestone year. The decade was young, there was new leadership in the White House, and the first astronauts were launched into space.

In Detroit, the era of fins and chrome had more or less run its course, and car makers were reducing the multiplicity of models as well as the weight and bulk of many of their cars. In the luxury field, Packard was now gone, leaving only three top contenders as the new decade began.

Cadillac was the premier American luxury car, the dominant postwar sales leader. Lincoln, a style-setter and racing champion in the early fifties, had, by 1960, fallen on leaner times. Imperial, a distant third in sales, was not a serious competitor in the luxury class until 1955, and had been struggling to main-

tain this slot ever since.

The American luxury car has traditionally emphasized big car room, a quiet, comfortable ride, quality appointments and finish, big engine performance and gadgetry. 1961 was no exception. All three luxury cars were powered by hefty V-8s. Each weighed close to 2½ tons unloaded, were 18 to 19 feet long, and carried a host of luxury features.

But 1961 was also something of a bellwether year. Lincoln, by reducing the size of its car by a foot and a half and adopting straighter, cleaner styling, departed from precedent. Cadillac, too,

chopped off a few inches, while retaining a more stylized version of its symbolic fins. Only Imperial remained the largest standard production American car, with even bigger fins than 1960 and some rather garish styling changes as well.

By today's standards, none of these cars is modest or compact, not even Lincoln. They represent a whole different era. Features you'd never find anymore seem to abound: the Imperial with its square steering wheel and push button transmission, the Lincoln with its suicide doors and reverse-opening hood, and Cadillac with every gadget imaginable — including power rear window vents.

The cars chosen for this comparison all hail from the heart of California's San Joaquin Valley. All are four-door models, each a well-maintained original

and frequently driven vehicle.

The Lincoln Continental four-door pillared sedan was offered only in one model. The Cadillac came in several different four-door models and styles, all hardtops. Our featured car is the top-of-the-line Fleetwood Sixty Special. Our test Imperial is the least expensive of three models in the Imperial line — the Custom four-door hardtop. There is a higher quality of leather and fabrics found in Lincoln and Cadillac interiors, but for all other purposes comparisons are about equal, as our Custom has a full complement of accessories and is mechanically the same as the more expensive Imperial Crown or LeBaron.

Lincoln

Of America's luxury cars for 1961, Lincoln was the most dramatically changed. Now available in just one series, the "Lincoln Continental," some 17 inches were trimmed from its length, 1½ inches from its width, three inches from its profile, and 200 pounds from its weight, in comparison to 1960 models. Some Buicks and Oldsmobiles were now actually larger.

The car was a new design. Although 1958 through 1960 Lincolns and Continentals were already quite square, the new Lincoln boasted slab sides, uncluttered with chrome or sculpturing and accented only by a peak moulding motif. A square, finless rear deck, "suicide"

rear doors, and a Thunderbird-inspired roof were also major components of the new look. Styling has become classic in the sense of long-lasting, and to the un-initiated, the '61 Continental can easily be mistaken for a much newer car.

Particularly unique are the rear doors, which open toward the back, allowing passengers to easily exit forward from the rear seat without having to slide around the door. The doors also include hardtop-style windows, without the frames of conventional-post sedans, yet with the post itself. The hood is hinged at the front like late fifties Fords, making engine access somewhat more difficult, though safer in the event the hood becomes unlatched while the car is in motion.

A little noted feature, after several years' absence on American cars, is the hood ornament. The Lincoln's four-pointed star was the first of a new generation of stand-up hood ornaments, not adopted by most American cars until the next decade.

On the inside, the Lincoln's use of chrome and light colors gives the car a sportier appearance. A white perforated headliner and a smaller steering wheel likewise give the illusion of greater interior room. Actually, due to its smaller outside dimensions, the Lincoln has the least inside space, including trunk room, of the big three. The front seat provides less room than Cadillac or Im-

perial, even with six-way electric adjustment. The steering wheel could use a tilt feature, not available until later years. Oddly, the T-Bird's swing-away wheel was not an option on Lincoln.

According to owner Tom Egger, the Lincoln is painted the original "Honey Beige," a very light beige with matching beige, almost white, pleated leather seats. Folding center armrests are available both front and rear, and the front seat backs have a very pleasing curved, semi-bucket design.

The dash is divided into passenger and driver sections, with a radio and ash receiver straddling the center between them. The speedometer is rather small, with gauges for fuel and temperature readings in a separate pod. The easy-to-operate air conditioning system is the best part of the dash. With one knob the A/C can be turned on and adjusted. Master controls for electric windows are located on the left arm rest panel, with a lock-out switch at the driver's command to keep little hands from playing with other windows. Vacuum operated door locks are controlled from another switch on the dash, and a dash light warns when a door is unlocked. Neither the window lockout or door lock safety light was offered by competing makes from GM or Chrysler at the time.

The fit and finish of the Lincoln are excellent, on par with Cadillac and better than Imperial. The Lincoln's body

Above and right: As with the rest of their styling, our three luxocars have very distinctive front end designs which identify them at a glance. Below: Windshield configurations, too, are quite different with more conservative Cadillac, left, and Lincoln, right, flanked by Imperial's massive expanse of glass.

SIA comparisonReport

feels tighter and more rattle free than the others, even after 124,000 miles, probably because it was the only luxury car in 1961 to utilize unit body construction.

In 1961 *Motor Trend* tests, however, the Lincoln proved to have the slowest acceleration of the three, despite having the largest engine in its class — some 430 cubic inches. In the 0-60 mph run, for example, the Lincoln was more than two seconds behind the rest. The heaviest car of the trio, Lincoln came only with a two-barrel carburetor, achieving slightly better fuel economy than its four-barrel comrades.

On the open road, the well-insulated Lincoln feels solid, with a firmer ride than Cadillac due to its shorter wheelbase and stiffer springing, but displaying some wallow in fast corners.

Overall, the Lincoln Continental for 1961 is an impressive car, sturdily built, tastefully designed and different in its own right.

Imperial

The original color on our featured Imperial is said to be "Malibu Tan." That's about the only modest statement we could find about the Imperial, and the paint is really more of a salmon pink.

Without a doubt, the Imperial is the most distinct of the three cars tested. This is not due to styling alone, although that is the biggest factor which makes the Imperial stand apart from the rest.

There is no middle ground with Imperial. People either like its flamboyant looks or see the car as an outrageous example of an era of "flim flam" and "excess."

This was not always the case. Until 1957 Imperial was one of the most conservative and understated American

1961 Cadillac, Imperial and Lincoln Performance Tests

Test	Cadillac	Imperial	Lincoln
Gas Mileage*	8-12 mpg	8-12 mpg	10-14 mpg
Acceleration*: 0-30 mph	3.8 sec.	3.7 sec.	4.7 sec.
0-45 mph	6.7 sec.	6.7 sec.	8.0 sec.
0-60 mph	10.4 sec.	10.5 sec.	12.9 sec.
Standing ¼-mile**	18.9 sec.	19.1 sec.	19.7 sec.
	78 mph	79 mph	75.5 mph
Braking Distances** From 30 mph	40 feet	41 feet	41 feet
From 60 mph	152 feet	185 feet	205 feet

* *Motor Trend*, May 1961 — Cadillac Sedan de Ville 4-dr; Imperial Crown 4-dr; Lincoln Continental 4-dr.

** *Motor Trend*, May 1962 — comparable '62 models. Cadillac Fleetwood 4-dr; Imperial LeBaron 4-dr; Lincoln Continental 4-dr.

luxury cars. Then, a new longer, lower design dominated by an immense greenhouse and sweeping rear fins was unveiled. Still, the new Imperial was attractive, and 1957 was a banner sales year for the marque.

From there, however, it was all downhill. The redesign of 1960 saw larger, less graceful fins and a "cow catcher"-like grille. As sales grew worse, styling became even more peculiar. 1961 was the ultimate in this respect, producing one of the worst sales records in Imperial's history.

Microphone-like taillamps hang from the underside of Imperial's higher and longer '61 fins. The front end is scooped out to allow the placement of four individual headlamp pods, harking back to headlamp designs of the thirties. The dash is pure science fiction, an almost square, elliptical steering wheel surrounded by two vertical pods of push buttons, one for the automatic trans-

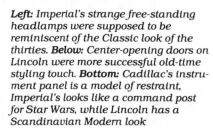

Left: Imperial's strange free-standing headlamps were supposed to be reminiscent of the Classic look of the thirties. Below: Center-opening doors on Lincoln were more successful old-time styling touch. Bottom: Cadillac's instrument panel is a model of restraint, Imperial's looks like a command post for Star Wars, while Lincoln has a Scandinavian Modern look

mission and the other for heater and air conditioning controls. Instrument lighting is electroluminescent, with green glowing dials and bright red needles.

Optional styling features for '61 included the "Flight Sweep" deck, with the imprint of a tire on the trunk lid, swivel front seats, and stainless steel roof inserts on some models. The whole effect made the extravagance of the '59 Cadillac pale by comparison.

Dimensions of the Imperial are huge, though no larger than the previous year's Lincoln or Cadillac. Still, at 19 feet in length, almost 82 inches wide, and a little taller than its rivals, Imperial is the largest, though not heaviest, of the '61s.

Notwithstanding its size, the Imperial's performance is on par with Cadillac, and its road handling character is better than both other makes. Negotiating a tight turn, Imperial feels more in control, though still not a sports car by any means. Torsion bar front suspension and stiffer rear springs helped to give Chrysler products a reputation for better handling for years. But there seems to be more wind and road noise from this 73,000-mile Imperial at cruising speed than its luxury counterparts.

In-town driving is another story. Due to its high fins and hulking size, the Imperial is a nightmare to parallel park,

and the car's wider turning circle makes U-turns on all but the broadest streets nearly impossible.

Space is, nevertheless, one of the virtues of this car. The trunk is the largest of the three, and seating the roomiest — some three inches more leg room front and back than Lincoln, and more than an inch greater than Cadillac in front. The engine is the most accessible

and easiest to service, and under the hood for '61 was the addition of an alternator, allowing the charging system to work even at idle. Other makes soon adopted it.

In spite of the strange-looking dash, Imperial is the only one of the big three with full readout instrumentation, and most controls are within easy reach of the driver. The square steering wheel is

Production Figures 1960-1969
Cadillac, Imperial and Lincoln

Year	Cadillac	Imperial	Lincoln
1960	142,184	17,719*	24,820**
1961	138,379	12,258*	25,164
1962	160,840	14,337	31,061
1963	163,174	14,121*	31,233
1964	165,959	23,295*	37,297
1965	181,435	18,409*	40,180
1966	196,675	13,742	54,755
1967	200,000	17,614	46,667
1968	230,003	15,361	39,134
1969	223,237	22,077	38,290
* includes Crown Ghia limousines			
** includes 11,086 Continentals			

Source: Langworth, Richard, *Encyclopedia of American Cars, 1940-1970*, Beekman House, 1980. Hendry, Maurice, *Cadillac, Standard of the World*, Complete 75 Year History, Automobile Quarterly Series, 1973.

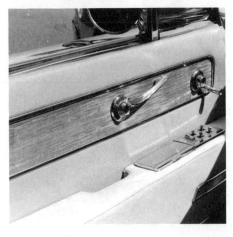

Left to right: Lincoln uses wood insert for decoration; Imp depends on different textures; Caddy employs a combination of wood and textures.

1961 Cadillac, Imperial and Lincoln Specifications

	CADILLAC	IMPERIAL	LINCOLN CONTINENTAL
Model	Fleetwood 4-dr hdtp.	Custom 4-dr hdtp.	4-dr sedan
Base price	$6,233	$5,109	$6,067
Engine	390 c.i.d. V-8	413 c.i.d. V-8	430 c.i.d. V-8
Bore and stroke	4.0 x 3.8	4.18 x 3.75	4.3 x 3.7
Compression	10.25:1	10.1:1	10:1
Carburetion	4-bbl	4-bbl	2-bbl
1961 horsepower	325 @ 4,800 rpm	350 @ 4,600 rpm	300 @ 4,100 rpm
Torque	430 @ 3,100 rpm	470 @ 2,800 rpm	465 @ 2,000 rpm
Transmission	Hydramatic 4-spd.	Torqueflite 3-spd.	TurboDrive 3-spd.
Driveshaft	Open 2 piece	Open 2 piece	Open needle roller bearing
Differential	Hypoid	Hypoid	Hypoid
Rear axle ratio	3.21:1	2.93:1	2.89:1
Suspension, front	Independent upper and lower control arms/ coil springs	Independent non-parallel control arms w/torsion bars and stabilizer bar	Independent upper and lower control arms, coil springs, and stabilizer bar
Suspension, rear	Coil springs	Non-independent semi-elliptic leaf springs	Non-independent semi-elliptic leaf springs
Steering	Power	Power	Power
Turns, lock to lock	3.7	3.5	3.7
Turn circle curb to curb	43 feet	48.2 feet	46.7 feet
Brakes	Power hydraulic self-adjusting	Power hydraulic	Power hydraulic self-adjusting
Lining area	203.74 square inches	251 square inches	227 square inches
Wheels and tires	15 inches	15 inches	14 inches
Factory specs	8.20 x 15	8.20 x 15	9.50 x 14
Body and frame	Separate body w/ tubular X frame	Separate body w/ double channel box frame and lateral cross members	Unitized body and frame w/torque box underbody
Curb weight	4,770 pounds	4,740 pounds	4,927 pounds
Length	222 inches	227.1 inches	212.4 inches
Width	79.8 inches	81.7 inches	78.6 inches
Height	56.3 inches	56.7 inches	53.5 inches
Wheelbase	129.5 inches	129.0 inches	123.0 inches
Ground clearance	5.3 inches	5.6 inches	5.5 inches
Front track	61 inches	61.8 inches	62.1 inches
Rear track	61 inches	62.2 inches	61.0 inches
Front seat dimensions Leg room Hip room Head room	45.6 inches 59.7 inches	46.9 inches 61.0 inches 38.9 inches	44.0 inches 59.7 inches 34.4 inches
Rear seat dimensions Leg room Hip room Head room	44.5 inches 63.0 inches	44.9 inches 60.2 inches 38.3 inches	40.7 inches 60.7 inches 33.6 inches
Trunk space		34.1 cubic feet	22.9 cubic feet

awkward for some, and the lack of a tilt feature restricts entry room when the wheel is not centered straight. The push button automatic transmission does not allow for a parking position, and the parking brake is the only way to keep the car from rolling away. Although other cars had a "Park" position on their automatic transmissions for years, it was not until 1963 that it was available on Imperial.

Power window controls are not as neatly concealed as on Lincoln or Cadillac, and switches are made of plastic, rather than chromed metal. The power seat switch, however, is the best of the three. Utilizing one large "ergonomic" knob, the driver simply turns the knob in the direction he wants the seat to go. There is no fumbling with multiple switches.

The Imperial makes no compromises. For its size, it's a superior handling and performing road car with styling few people appreciate.

Cadillac

Dave Jolliff of Modesto must like Cadillacs; he owns six of them including the subject of this article, a 97,000-mile Fleetwood in factory "Tunis Beige" colors.

Styling of the '61 Cadillac was both new and different. There was an all-new body, a few inches shorter, a little narrower, with improved insulation, wider door openings, better steering geometry, and other refinements. In keeping with Cadillac thinking, however, styling changes were modest. Traditional themes — the taillamp fins, the massive mesh grille, and the ever-famous "V" crest, albeit of a more razor-edge design, were all recognizably Cadillac.

From today's perspective, Lincoln appears the most conservative of the '61 luxury cars. But in 1961, it was actually Cadillac which was the least changed, from the standpoint of styling. Cadillac was still a Cadillac.

This was due to a philosophy of year-to-year styling continuity — never so many changes you couldn't recognize a new Cadillac. This helped to maintain

Left: Lincoln engine originally was designed for use in Edsel Citation. **Below left:** *Imperial had highest bhp rating at 350.* **Below:** *Cadillac's 390-c.i.d. V-8 was smallest of the trio. None were a joy for service access.* **Bottom:** *Cadillac wins the trunk space contest.*

the resale value of older Cadillacs as well. Perhaps that is why, with the abandonment of a creed which served it well for so many years, Cadillac has now run into trouble in the eighties era of downsizing.

On the road, the '61 Cadillac is the quietest and smoothest riding of the three cars. Performance from its 390-c.i.d. V-8 was 1/10th of a second faster than Imperial at 0-60 in 1961 *Motor Trend* tests of similar models, and at high speed Cadillac virtually floats down the highways and byways.

But steering is so light, there's practically no feel. This can be especially disconcerting at highway speeds when the driver may wonder whether anything is attached to the other end of the column. Cornering at rapid pace is also not one of the Cad's better qualities, although brakes proved most worthy, stopping from 60 mph in comparable *Motor Trend* tests 33 feet sooner than an Imperial LeBaron and more than 50 feet better than Lincoln.

On the inside, Cadillac really shines. The dash is richer looking than competitors, with handsome chrome accents and a detailed two-tone steering wheel. Wheel position is also the most comfortable of the three, even for large folks. The best feature is the accessibility of the controls, especially on Cadillac's left door panel, from which you can operate all electric windows and vents, door locks, the six-way power seat and remote outside left mirror from the arm

Cadillac's fins had come somewhat down to earth by '61; Lincoln eschewed them altogether; Imperial was going for a new altitude record for their fins.

All Model Comparison
1961 Luxury Cars

Model	Weight	Price	Production
CADILLAC			
Series 62			
2-door hardtop coupe	4,560 pounds	$4,892	16,005
4-door hardtop 6-window	4,680 pounds	$5,080	26,216
4-door hardtop 4-window	4,660 pounds	$5,080	4,700
2-door convertible	4,720 pounds	$5,455	15,500
Chassis			5
DeVille			
2-door hardtop coupe	4,595 pounds	$5,252	20,156
4-door hardtop 6-window	4,710 pounds	$5,498	26,415
4-door hardtop 4-window	4,715 pounds	$5,498	4,847
4-door town sedan		$5,498	3,756
Fleetwood Sixty Special			
4-door hardtop sedan*	4,770 pounds	$6,233	15,500
Eldorado Biarritz			
2-door convertible		$6,477	1,450
Series 75 (149.8" wheelbase)			
4-door sedan, 9 passenger	5,390 pounds	$9,533	699
4-door limo, 9 passenger	5,420 pounds	$9,748	926
Commercial chassis (156" wheelbase)			2,204
Total			138,379
IMPERIAL			
Custom			
2-door hardtop coupe	4,715 pounds	$4,923	889
4-door hardtop sedan*	4,740 pounds	$5,109	4,129
Crown			
2-door hardtop coupe	4,790 pounds	$5,403	1,007
4-door hardtop sedan	4,855 pounds	$5,647	4,769
4-door convertible	4,865 pounds	$5,774	429
LeBaron			
4-door hardtop sedan	4,875 pounds	$6,426	1,026
Crown Ghia Limousine (149.5" wheelbase)			
4-door limo, 9 passenger	5,960 pounds	$16,500	9
Total			12,258
LINCOLN CONTINENTAL			
4-door sedan*	4,927 pounds	$6,067	22,307
4-door convertible sedan	5,215 pounds	$6,713	2,857
Total			25,164

* models tested

Source: Langworth, *Encyclopedia of American Cars, 1940-70*, Beekman. Hendry, Maurice, *Cadillac, Standard of the World*. Complete 75 year history. Automobile Quarterly Series, 1973.

SIA comparisonReport

rest — without hardly moving your wrist. Getting used to which switch controls what is the only drawback.

Cadillac interior room is superior to Lincoln and close to Imperial both front and back. Entry and exit are improved by wider opening doors and the elimination of the previous year's windshield "dogleg."

Cadillac is brimming with luxury gadgets: an electric eye "hi-lo" headlamp beam changer, electric rear venti-panes, hand straps and assist handles on seats and door panels, and the renowned remote and pull-down electric trunk lid, among others.

The patterned upholstery cloth is well-tailored but not as first cabin as one might expect to find in a car of Fleetwood's genre, nor as elegant as the broadcloth and leather interior of comparable Imperial LeBarons.

Cadillac also skimps on instrumentation, providing idiot lights instead of analog gauges for most functions; typical of GM cars of the time. One last but probably irrelevant criticism: The engine compartment is the least accessible of the cars in its class; the engine and air conditioning apparatus are crammed into a small compartment. Cadillac owners, on the other hand, can probably afford to let the mechanic

*Above: With six-way seats and generous room in all directions, nearly any driver can be comfortable in all three cars. **Below:** Cadillac's flashiest looks are out back. Imperial's rear is as wild as the front. Lincoln looks understated, well balanced.*

worry about that.

Generally speaking, the 1961 Cadillac best combines those elements which people seem to want most in a luxury car: performance; a smooth, quiet ride; and elegant luxury.

All three luxury cars for 1961 are worthy automobiles representing an era which many regret has passed, an era which offered both driver and passengers the feeling of power, prestige, luxury and security in a big car package.

To evaluate which car is superior would be difficult. Each has its own qualities: the Cadillac with the best ride and most luxury appointments, the Imperial the best handling road car, and the Lincoln the best looking and most solid feeling.

But the most striking qualities of all three are their differences. Unlike similarly styled cars of today, there is no mistaking one for another — or for a Chevrolet for that matter. From the refined Lincoln to the bizarre Imperial, and a Cadillac that looks like a Cadillac should, each American luxury car of the early sixties had its own distinctive identity. □

1966 Oldsmobile Toronado vs. 1967 Cadillac Eldorado
The Front Line of Front-Wheel Drive

by John F. Katz
photos by Vince Wright

IN the spring of 1965, front-wheel drive was still weird science. Saabs had it, and Citroëns, and Minis, and DKW's, and maybe a few other foreign compacts that most Americans had never seen. The last big US car to crawl forward on front-wheel power had been the Cord, and the man in the proverbial street could tell you that the Cord had failed financially, although he probably couldn't tell you why.

By the fall of 1965, however, the Oldsmobile Toronado had proven not only that front-wheel drive could work in a full-size automobile, but that it delivered real-world improvements in handling, traction, and interior room. The

press heralded the Toronado as the vanguard of a new generation—a prediction seemingly confirmed by the appearance of the front-wheel-driven Cadillac Eldorado in 1967.

Then a dozen years of silence followed before Detroit released another big front-drive automobile, leaving the Toronado and Eldorado alone in a class of two.

The Front-Drive Initiative
General Motors had exhibited a couple of front-wheel-drive show cars in the fifties, but the real inspiration for the Toronado came from an experimental *rear*-drive chassis. In 1956-57, GM launched an ambitious program to convert its 1960-model full-size cars to a front-engine, rear-transaxle configuration. With engines growing larger and heavier, the so-called "Q" chassis promised better traction by shifting the weight of the transmission to the rear. But the projected cost of production shelved the project permanently. That's when Andrew K. Watt, who headed Advanced Engineering at Oldsmobile, sug-

Left: *Like its Cord front-drive predecessor, Toronado used hide-away headlamps. Eldo sported conventional quads to harmonize with eggcrate grille.* **Above and below:** *Both cars measured over six and one-half feet wide and horizontal styling themes helped emphasize this fact.*

gested front-wheel drive as an alternative. Corporate Engineering Staff clearly wasn't interested (at least not at first), but Watt found enthusiastic support within the Olds division from general manager Jack Wolfram as well as chief engineer Harold Metzel and his assistant, John B. Beltz.

Development problems were political as much as technical. Already, corporate management was pressuring the divisions to design more common components into their full-sized models. Beltz thought a front-drive compact stood a better chance of slipping past the bean counters—and if it didn't, he could always point to the even more anomalous Chevrolet Corvair. Watt had a small prototype running by the spring of 1960, based on the soon-to-be-released F-85, but with its 215-c.i.d. V-8 turned sideways, and dual-stage chain drive to its front wheels. Olds engineers later tried gears and even steel-reinforced belts but ultimately returned to chain drive as the best compromise between quiet and durability.

Meanwhile, however, market research began to confirm what Chevrolet dealers already suspected: that compact car buyers didn't particularly like technical innovation. The budding "personal luxury" market looked more promising, so that's where Beltz and Watt re-directed their efforts.

In 1961-62, they tested a series of highly modified Olds 88s, with unit construction and transversely mounted 394-c.i.d. V-8s driving the front wheels. To clear space for the driveshafts between the front suspension arms, they experimented with coil springs on the upper arms and with short, laminated torsion bars, before settling on long, solid torsion bars that anchored to a crossmember under the front seat. They also developed a narrow-profile planetary differential, which not only saved space but reduced steering feedback by minimizing friction. Early versions carried their engines on short front stub frames, but too much noise and too little stiffness led to a sub frame that extended all the way back to the rear seat. The final Toronado structure would boast twice the torsional stiffness of the perimeter-framed Ninety-Eight.

Olds engineers Jim Lewis and Howard Kehrl designed the definitive driveline. They split a standard Turbo-HydraMatic transmission in half, leaving its variable-pitch torque converter bolted up to the back of the engine, but turning the gearbox around 180 degrees and tucking it under the left bank of cylinders. That way, the converter damped out periodic torque peaks before they reached the chain that drove the gearbox. The driving sprocket itself was rubber damped, allowing two degrees of free movement.

A short, rigid shaft passed from the planetary differential on the left, under a special humped oil pan, to a bearing on the right, so the left and right half-shafts were equal in length. (Earlier on, Olds had tried running the shaft *through* the oil pan, but abandoned this idea as unnecessarily costly.) The pan itself required some close engineering attention, to get the oil to flow up over the hump without foaming. Four Rzeppa constant-velocity joints permitted the half shafts to follow the movements of the wheels, while a single rubber coupling in the right-side shaft allowed seven degrees of free rotation, again to dampen vibration.

Having sunk a considerable sum of

money into the front end, the engineers wanted to keep the rear suspension as simple and inexpensive a possible. The rear axle was nothing more than a stamped, hat-section beam suspended on two single-leaf springs. A second set of shock absorbers, mounted horizontally, dampened braking torque without adding ride harshness.

To maintain balance with the transmission alongside the engine, Olds pushed the engine itself 1.82 inches to the right of the car's centerline, and positioned most of its mass behind the front axle. Despite its impressive front overhang, the production Toronado would carry two-thirds of its weight inside its wheelbase.

The Toronado's rigid body structure allowed the stiffest springs in the industry: 162 lb./in. in front, nearly twice the spring rate of Oldsmobile's own sporty Starfire; and 157 lb./in. in the rear. Working with Firestone, Olds developed a special "TFD" (Toronado Front Drive) tire with a tread pattern designed to enhance wet traction and a higher cord angle to stiffen the sidewalls. (Later on, Uniroyal also produced TFD's, and Goodyear radials became an option.)

Olds division demonstrated the mechanical package to corporate management at the Desert Proving Ground in Mesa, Arizona, in February 1964, where Beltz sold the idea to an initially skeptical Ed Cole (then v.p. of the car and truck divisions). But GM's notoriously conservative president, John F. Gordon, approved a front-drive, personal-luxury coupe for Oldsmobile only if it shared a body shell with the Buick Riviera.

Oldsmobile pulls ahead...

Had it sat squarely upon a box-stock 88 chassis, the Toronado would have been remembered for its outstanding styling alone. "The idea about the Toro-

Top and opposite bottom: Toro and Eldo have almost identical handling characteristics. Only difference on test cars was better grip of radials on Toronado. *Above right and right:* Olds's slotted wheel covers add practical touch. Eldo wheel covers are more in character with traditional Cadillac style. *Facing page, center:* Eldorado's stiletto taillamp treatment finishes off the car perfectly. A/C intake slots are in Caddy's rear fenders.

nado that was very new," explained David R. Holls, then chief of the Buick studio, "was that the roof shape merged with the side and went all the way down to the exaggerated fender forms. That had been done before on the Valiant, but not nearly as dramatically."

Charles M. Jordan, Cadillac studio chief from 1958 and corporate director of Design from 1962, recalled how the Toronado went from "concept right through to production" with minimal alteration. "Some designs are hard to come by, and you don't quite get it. But in the case of the Toronado there was only one design. It almost never happens that way."

The concept that became the Toronado was born purely as a design exercise in mid-1962. "We had just come through two years of meat-and-potatoes design work," recalled Olds studio chief Stan Wilen, "the kinds of things that really tighten designers up. I could see that we needed some creative rejuvenation. So I posed the problem: 'I would like to do a Riviera-type car for Oldsmobile.' Of course we had seen the ['63] Riviera when it was in clay. Dave North, my assistant, came up with this flaming red car."

Wilen said that he wasn't seriously planning to create a Riviera competitor, at least not in the beginning. But "the

Riviera showed that there was a fairly lucrative market, and Olds was interested. They were competitive divisions; they sold to much the same customer in much the same price class." North's design survived the transition from sketch to full-size rendering, and that's when it was noticed by Cole and Design v.p. Bill Mitchell. "And Cole, as he walked out of the studio, said to Mitchell, 'You know, we're talking about a front-drive version of that car.' I was called into a meeting the next day, and we were told to fit it over a current ['63-65] Riviera underbody.... And it survived. It still looked pretty good."

Wilen's team produced a scale model, and then Mitchell assigned Advanced Studio 3 to shape the full-size clay. But

the car returned to Olds for finishing touches. Management saw the clay in February 1963, and sent it back for a higher roof and a longer trunk. Final approval came in April.

Beltz, who had by then succeeded Metzel as chief engineer, demanded performance to match the new car's looks. Oldsmobile's 425-c.i.d. V-8, new for 1965, produced 370 bhp in the Jetstar I and Starfire. But Beltz wanted 385 bhp, which his staff delivered via freer-breathing heads and a higher-lift, longer-duration cam. A special low-profile intake manifold, necessitated by the exceptionally low hood, didn't seem to hurt performance any.

Camouflaged prototypes hit the road in October 1964. As late as 1965, how-

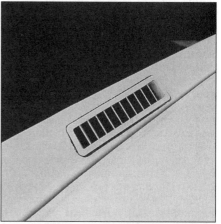

ever, Olds marketing was still busy rejecting names for them. At that time the "Toronado" label belonged to Chevrolet, having appeared on a little-noted 1963 show car. Then Chevrolet general manager Bunkie Knudsen followed Cole into the Olds studio one day, where Cole asked if the front-drive car had a name yet. When the answer was negative, Bunkie casually suggested "Toronado...We're not using it."

Thirty-seven pilot-production Toronados were running by May, and full-scale production commenced in September. Bobby Unser pushed (pulled?) a Toronado up Pikes Peak in 14 minutes, 9.9 seconds, more than a minute behind the stock-car record that Parnelli Jones has set in a Mercury, but quick enough to show the skeptics that front-drivers could climb hills. When *Car and Driver* tested a Toronado in November '65, it generated the highest lateral acceleration they had ever recorded for a full-size American car. Then *Motor Trend* named the Toronado Car of the Year, adding that "never in the 14-year history of this award had the choice been so obvious and unanimous." In fact, the press as a whole responded ecstatically to the Toronado's room, comfort, and roadability—and grumbled only quietly about its barely adequate brakes.

Olds sold 40,963 Toronados in the 1966 model year, which was hardly a bad start for a brand-new, fairly radical and expensive car. Still, that was about 9,000 Toronados short of Lansing's expectations. The mildly face-lifted '67 addressed the braking problem with a standard front-to-rear proportioning valve and optional Corvette front discs, but sales plunged to 21,790. The designers were told to make future Toronados more conventional. "They wanted the other Oldses, which were doing well in the market, to rub off on it, to give it some confidence," said Wilen. But the Toronado barely tread water until the early seventies, when it was re-cast entirely as an upright, baroque, and conservative luxury coupe that just happened to be front-wheel-driven.

...and Cadillac follows

As early as 1961, and possibly earlier, GM's corporate Engineering Staff appears to have tested a front-drive prototype of its own, powered by a Cadillac V-8. But the front-drive '67 Eldorado was created by Design Staff to fit the mechanical package developed by Oldsmobile. Cadillac Division hardly had anything to do with it.

"They couldn't care less," remarked Jordan. "It didn't come from the division, and it wasn't asked for by the mar-

Above and right: Toronado's styling was totally clean-sheet from front to back. Eldorado retained traditional Cadillac badge and laurel wreath.
Facing page: Oldsmobile's dashboard layout and steering wheel styling were just as fresh as rest of car. Eldorado again followed more established Cadillac look.

keting guys." But ever since the demise of the original Eldorado Brougham, Design Staff had an Advanced studio "working on this idea of doing a sporty-elegant Cadillac—a tighter, more lively, more youthful Cadillac. We produced a few full-size designs and clay models, but we never could sell it to the corporation. It wasn't until the architecture for the Toronado was born that we saw this opportunity of doing a sporty-elegant Cadillac as a coupe."

"I don't think Cadillac was promoting it so much as Bill Mitchell was," confirmed Holls. "How could you let Buick and Oldsmobile have this special car and Cadillac have nothing? So whether Cadillac liked it or not, Design Staff sold that Eldorado. Ed Cole was behind it."

In *Cadillac, Standard of the World,* Maurice Hendry unearthed a remarkable design study from 1962, a true missing link with the near-fully developed roofline, fender lines, hood, grille, and body-side cross-section of the production '67 Eldorado; combined with almost Toronado-like round wheel openings; and short suicide doors for the

rear passengers, like the old Eldorado Brougham. "Maybe six, seven months after we started," Wilen remembered, "Cadillac was already on the trail. We provided them with drawings of our wheels, which were special because of the tendency for the brakes to overheat, and also our driveline layout, our firewall, etc. Chuck Jordan was their chief designer then, and of course he was going to make his car the classiest of the three." The definitive two-door hardtop was finished by May 1964. But the radical-looking Cadillac fought a hard battle for acceptance at both the corporate and divisional level.

According to Holls, Cole slipped the Eldorado clay past Gordon when the president wasn't ready to give it his full attention. "He saw it, but it never really hit. He'd seen too much that day, and didn't know what he was looking at. So Cole said to get it out of the studio and hide it." He didn't want to give Gordon a chance to change his mind. But by the time that approval came, said Jordan, Cadillac had lost critical months to Oldsmobile. "We did it as fast as we

Specifications: '66 Oldsmobile Toronado vs. '67 Cadillac Eldorado

	Oldsmobile	Cadillac
Base price	$4,585	$6,277
Price as tested (est.)	$5,365	$7,630
Engine	V-8	V-8
Bore x stroke	4.13 inches x 3.97 inches	4.13 inches x 4.00 inches
Displacement	425 cubic inches	429 cubic inches
Compression ratio	10.5:1	10.5:1
Horsepower @ rpm	385 @ 4,800 (gross)	340 @ 4,600 (gross)
Torque/rpm	475 @ 3,200 (gross)	480 @ 3,000 (gross)
Taxable horsepower	54.6	54.6
Valve configuration	Ohv	Ohv
Valve lifters	Hydraulic	Hydraulic
Main bearings	5	5
Carburetor	1 Rochester 4-bbl	1 Rochester 4-bbl
Fuel system	Mechanical pump	Mechanical pump
Lubrication	Pressure	Pressure
Cooling	Centrifugal pump	Centrifugal pump
Exhaust system	Dual with single transverse muffler, dual outlets	Dual with single transverse muffler, single outlet
Electrical system	12-volt	12-volt
Transmission	Three-speed automatic with torque converter	
Max. converter ratio	2.20:1	2.20:1
Gear ratios	1st: 2.48:1; 2nd: 1.48:1; 3rd: 1.00:1; Reverse: 2.08:1	
Drive axle	Spiral-bevel ring and pinion, planetary differential, open drive shafts with four Rzeppa-type constant-velocity joints	
Ratio	3.21:1	3.21:1
Steering gear	Recirculating ball w/integral hydraulic servo, plus hydraulic damper	
Ratio (overall)	17.8:1 (constant)	14.1–16.3:1 (variable)
Turns lock-to-lock	3.4	2.75
Turning circle	43 feet	41 feet
Brakes	Four-wheel hydraulic with vacuum servo, finned iron drums	
Drum size	11 x 2.75 front; 11 x 2.00 rear	12 x 2.75 front; 12 x 2.00 rear
Swept area	328.2 sq. in.	358.0 sq. in.
Parking brake	Mechanical, on rear drums	Mechanical, on rear drums
Construction	Unit body with 3/4-length sub-frame	
Front suspension	Independent, unequal-length A-arms, torsion bars, link-type anti-roll bar	
Rear suspension	Beam axle on single-leaf springs, pneumatic leveling on Cadillac only	
Shock absorbers, front rear	Double-acting hydraulic, one per wheel Double-acting hydraulic, one vertical and one horizontal per wheel	
Tires	Michelin X 225 x 15	General 9.15 x 15
Wheels	Stamped steel, 15 x 6JK	Stamped steel, 15 x 6JK
Wheelbase	119.0 inches	120.0 inches
Overall length	211.0 inches	221.0 inches
Overall width	78.5 inches	80.0 inches
Overall height (empty)	52.8 inches	53.3 inches
Front track	63.5 inches	63.5 inches
Rear track	63.0 inches	63.0 inches
Min. road clearance	5.0 inches	5.4 inches
Curb weight	4,496 pounds	4,950 pounds
Weight distribution, f/r	60.3/39.7	58.0/42.0
Crankcase capacity	6 quarts w/filter	5 quarts w/filter
Cooling system capacity	17.5 quarts	18.6 quarts
Fuel tank	24 gallons	24 gallons
Transmission oil capacity	24 pints	24 pints
Differential oil capacity	4 pints	4 pints
Stroke/bore ratio	0.961	0.968
Lb./c.i.d.	0.91	0.79
Lb./bhp	11.7	14.6
Lb./sq. in. brake area	13.7	13.8
Performance: * 0-60	9.5 seconds	8.9 seconds
1/4-mile	17.2 seconds @ 82 mph	17.0 @ 84 mph
Braking, 60-0	167 feet	204 feet

* Test figures from *Motor Trend*. Toronado tested December 1965; Eldorado tested January 1957

could and still couldn't get it out until a year later than the Toronado."

Despite its common cowl and windshield, the Eldorado looked radically different from its Oldsmobile progenitor. It started with the basic proportions: The Eldorado measured eleven inches longer than the Olds, with ten of those inches behind the rear wheels. And where the Toronado set a new style for future Oldsmobiles to follow, the Eldorado drew heavily from Cadillac tradition.

The Cadillac designers deliberately kept a more conservative note in the interior as well. "We were thrilled, mesmerized by the idea of doing a flat floor in a coupe," said Jordan. "The Toronado was a very progressive design, a leader in technology, and we tried to express that quality...in the interior. But the Cadillac was still very much a Cadillac, and the interior reflected that philosophy." Interestingly, Cadillac claimed only five-passenger capacity for the Eldo, while Olds billed the Toronado as a six-seater.

Nor was the Eldorado an exact mechanical duplicate of the Toronado. Its 429-c.i.d. engine was standard issue for Cadillacs at that time, although it was fitted with a modified oil pan and mated to an unaltered Toronado driveline. Cadillac tuned the Eldorado suspension for a softer ride, and added pneumatic self-leveling and faster, variable-ratio power steering.

The Eldorado was not as warmly received by the press. The magazines

SIA comparisonReport

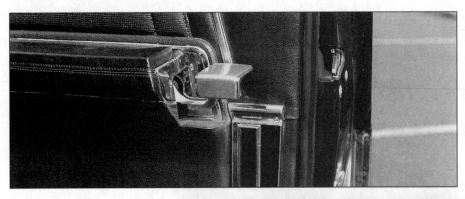

complained about understeer and what *Car and Driver* termed "pitiful" brakes. *Car Life* tested an Eldorado with the optional front discs and found it still took longer to stop than a drum-braked Calais. But none of this seemed to bother some 17,930 buyers during the Eldorado's inaugural model year. That was a modest number of cars, but Cadillac had projected only 15,000 sales—and the Eldo was capturing the youngest 10 percent of Cadillac buyers, exactly as intended. Sales expanded to 24,582 in 1968 and then held steady while the Toronado fumbled for its niche.

Driving Impressions

The late Alex Tremulis once characterized '66 Toronado as "homage to four exposed wheels." It remains an apt description, but to my eye the Toronado is more striking than truly beautiful, suffering in the inevitable comparison against its curvier, sexier sister, the Buick Riviera. The sharp-finned Eldorado, on the other hand, invites comparison only with other Cadillacs, and in that contest it cannot lose. With its wall-to-wall grille and razor-edge lines, '67 Eldorado is the distilled essence of Cadillac, the Cadillac that Cadillac had been striving to achieve since 1955 (at least)—and the one they have never since equaled.

Interior ambiance is as strikingly different as exterior style. Oldsmobile designed the whole front compartment of the Toronado to emphasize the extra space afforded by front-wheel drive, with a boldly flattened dash and a floating, rectangular instrument

---

Competition From Flint: The Buick Riviera

If GM management had had its way, the '66 Riviera would have shared not just the Toronado body shell, but its front-wheel-driveline as well. After all, part of the idea behind the Toronado (and Eldorado, too) was to absorb some of the cost of manufacturing the Riviera. But Buick Division, finally on a comeback after some very dark years in the late fifties, balked at the untried concept. "The '63 Riviera was a terrific car," Dave Holls commented, "and they had no reason to change that."

For a while, Buick stalled E-body development while its engineers proved that they could fit the common body over the Riviera's full-length cruciform frame and rear-wheel driveline. (They not only succeeded but saved nearly 200 pounds in the process!) Ultimately, the extensively redesigned '66 Riviera shared the cowl, windshield, and roof panel of the Toronado; according to some sources, the clever Buick body men even salvaged some common stampings in the floor. At one time the two cars were to share door skins too, but in the end only the inner door structure was common between them.

We wondered if the need to share a roof with the Toronado dictated the fastback form of the '66 Riviera, but Chuck Jordan assured us that it did not. Holls, he said, was already sketching racier Rivieras, and "we wanted to get away from the Rolls-Royce razor-edge of the '63."

The '67 Riviera looked hardly any different from the '66, but packed a larger, more powerful engine; and more powerful standard drum brakes, with vented front discs as an option. Alone among personal luxury coupes, the Riviera offered a handling option: the GS package, which added faster steering, firmer suspension, and a shorter-geared Positraction rear. This gave the Buick a distinct advantage when *Motor Trend* tested a Riviera, Toronado, and Eldorado against a Pontiac Grand Prix and a Ford Thunderbird in August 1967. The Rivvie out-ran its intramural brethren and the big-engined 'Bird, with no excessive noise or mechanical fuss. And it tied with the Toronado for the best ride and handling.

Stan Wilen nicely summed up the styling relationship of the three GM E-bodies: "There was kind of a masculine, brutal touch to the Olds, a silky, fluid look to the Riviera, and the Eldorado was tailored, elegant." Mostly, it was a matter of which one you liked.

	1966 Riviera	1967 Riviera
Base price	$4,424	$4,469
Price as tested	$5,503	$5,512
Engine	V-8, ohv	V-8, ohv
Bore x stroke	4.3125 x 3.64 in.*	4.19 x 3.90 in.
Displacement	425 cu. in.	430 cu. in.
Comp. ratio	10.25:1	10.25:1
Bhp @ rpm (gross)	340 @ 4,400	360 @ 5,000
Torque @ rpm (gross)	465 @ 2,800	475 @ 3,200
Carburetion	1 x 4 bbl	1 x 4 bbl
Final drive ratio	3.23:1	3.42:1
Steering		
Turns lock-to-lock	4.0	3.57
Turning circle	44.0 ft.	42.3 ft.
Brakes f/r	Drum/Drum	Drum/Drum
Construction	Separate body on X-shaped backbone frame	
Front susp.	Independent, coil springs	
Rear susp.	Live axle, coil springs	
Tires	8.45 x 15	8.45 x 15
Wheelbase	119.0 in.	119.0 in.
Overall length	211.2 in.	211.3 in.
Overall width	78.8 in.	79.4 in.
Overall height (empty)	53.4 in	53.2 in.
Front track	63.5 in.	63.5 in.
Rear track	63.0 in.	63.0 in.
Curb weight	4,400 lb.	4,420 lb.
Performance*		
0-60	8.6 sec	7.8 sec
1/4-mile	16.4 sec @ 84 mph	15.9 @ 86 mph
Braking, 60-0	154 ft.	165 ft.
Production	45,348	42,799

*from *Motor Trend*, '66 GS tested February 1966; '67 GS tested August 1967.

Facing page, top: Big Toro doors may be opened from either end. **Below:** *Caddy's electrical controls are all within a thumb-flick of the driver.* **Above:** *Two quite different styling approaches to a large front-drive coupe. You want curves or do you want angles?*

pod. Big, red-needled gauges flank a rolling-drum speedometer — science fiction in the sixties. It's as dazzling as the Starship Enterprise, and yet as logical as Mr. Spock, with all controls well-organized and readily within reach.

The Eldorado's relatively conservative dash, by comparison, lacks not only an ammeter but imagination — although I'd have to admit that it works nearly as well.

In both cars, a "Strato-Bench" seat features individual, bucket-like backrests. These support the low back nicely, but taper off in the shoulder area, a design pleasant to the eye but not to the spine. The Eldorado's optional six-way power adjustment helps compensate somewhat, although no matter where I put it, I felt as though I was sitting lower than in the Toronado, and peering out over a longer hood.

Beyond styling, however, very little separates these corporate cousins. Our featured Toronado enjoyed a slight edge in ride and handling, probably because it has been fitted with radial tires. (Before anyone cries foul, recall that by 1967 the Toronado could be ordered with radials, while the Eldorado could not.) Still, never before — not even when I sampled two Chevrolet 409s for *SIA* #163 — have I come away from a comparisonReport feeling so much as though I'd driven the same car twice.

Their engines even sound the same: a heavily muffled V-8 rattle, higher in tone than I expected from such large-displacement mills. Both cars accelerate very smoothly, and the split Turbo-

HydraMatic upshifts imperceptibly even at full throttle. Both sprint more impressively from 50-75 than from 0-50. Despite its more favorable power-to-weight ratio, the Toronado feels only marginally quicker, but notice that the rated torque of the two engines is nearly the same. Neither car is as quick as its

muscular power rating would suggest, proving that pounds can absorb a lot of ponies.

The Toronado's steering wheel is a wonderful thing, a deep-dished, four-spoke affair suggesting the control yoke of a small plane, and yet the perfect handle for holding an automobile. The

The comparisonReport Cars

We feel extremely fortunate to have found two absolutely original cars for our comparison, living within 50 miles of each other in eastern Pennsylvania.

Our featured '66 Toronado was purchased new by Elbert Van Orden, who said he "had to have it" the moment he saw it at Brogan Cadillac-Oldsmobile in Paterson, New Jersey. It is a "deluxe" model, which means it has individual, bucket-style backrests for its bench front seat, a second set of interior door handles positioned for the rear-seat passengers, and trim rings on its wheels. Beyond that, it is equipped with air conditioning, tinted glass, deluxe seat belts and an AM radio with a rear-seat speaker. I was particularly surprised to find manually cranked windows in such an exotic luxury machine.

Shortly after he bought it, Van Orden replaced the Toronado's Firestone TFD 8.85 x 15 tires with equivalent-sized 225 x 15 Michelin X radials. He drove the car infrequently, and only in good weather, and had rolled up only 37,000 miles when he sold it in 1994 to his close friend Ray Lemmon. Mr. Van Orden drove down from his current home in Shushan, New York (not far across the border from *SIA* headquarters in Vermont), to attend our photo session.

By contrast, our '67 Eldorado is loaded with options, including six-way power seats, power rear windows (all Eldos came with power front windows and four-way power seats), cruise control, tilt-and-telescope steering wheel, automatic climate control, AM-FM stereo, remote trunk release, vinyl roof, Twilight Sentinel and Guide-Matic power headlight dimmer. It was first registered to an engineer in California, who was transferred to Germany less than a year later. He took his Eldorado with him, enjoyed two or three years in the land of Frie Fahrt, and then brought it home again to California. It passed through the hands of just one other owner before Dave Broadway bought it in 1989, and drove it back to Pennsylvania from Scottsdale, Arizona. Its odometer read 35,094 on the day of our drive.

When Dave bought the car, it had been modified with European-spec headlights and radial tires. The former tended to overload the high-beam relay, and the latter were not available on first-year Eldorados, so Dave dutifully switched back to dim-glowing T3s and period bias-ply Generals. But he left the German-language manufacturer's tag (apparently required by German law) on the inside right front fender.

steering column is oddly skewed to the center of the car, but I think I'd get used to that with time. By comparison the Eldo's tiny wheel feels too fragile and dainty for such a large machine. I also preferred the Oldsmobile's somewhat slower-geared, constant-ratio steering to the very fast variable-ratio box in the Cadillac—although both cars could benefit from more road feel.

And even the lighter Toronado feels ponderous in turns, with more body roll than I expected given its high spring rates. Understeer, on the other hand, is well under control; in fact the Toro doesn't feel quite as nose-heavy as most big rear-drive cars from the same era.

The Eldorado handles about the same—just add 500 pounds. And not surprisingly, its overworked bias-ply booties hiss and squeal at lower speeds than the Toronado's more sophisticated radials. Both cars, even the softer-sprung Eldorado, ride stiffly for full-size US iron; and the Cadillac, particularly, thumps hard over the seams in a concrete roadway. Again, however, the Caddy's ride harshness could be easily attributed to its bias-ply tires. Both cars float slightly at the front end, as if their springs were too firm for their shocks.

So (surprise!) neither of these front-drive behemoths would be the ideal partner for a twisty-road tango—yet either would make a splendid companion for cross-country travel. How would

Competition from Dearborn: The Ford Thunderbird

Ironically, the Thunderbird came squeakingly close to being front-wheel driven as well, with a mechanical package that looked suspiciously similar to the Toronado's. Ford spent $3 million in the late fifties to develop a front-wheel-drive layout for the '61 T-Bird; the program was first delayed until '62 (while the new styling appeared on-time) and then abandoned entirely. The 'Bird hardly needed the additional expense of front-wheel drive, reasoned management, when its high, bulky console was already part of its identity.

It seems very unlikely that Ford's front-drive program could have swayed GM, but the Toronado's styling appears to have influenced Ford. Dave Holls claims that the Toronado design was leaked to Dearborn, and that Ford stylists actually modeled the car full-size as a study for the '67 Thunderbird. That would certainly explain some extremely Toronado-like clays that kicked around the Ford studios in 1964. Their legacy can be seen in the final product, in the vertical edges of the front fenders, and (on the two-door) in the gentle transition of the roof into the lower body.

This was a time of change for the T-Bird. The '66 model was the last descendant of the original "Squarebird," still unit-bodied, and sharing its cowl, windshield, and other components with the Lincoln Continental. Whereas the '67 was a different 'Bird altogether, with a separate body on a shortened Ford frame. Two-door models grew from 113 to 115 inches in wheelbase, and Ford now offered a four-door variant on a 117-inch chassis. But even the new four-door weighed a little less than the old unit-body coupe, and the Thunderbird, while hardly small, remained the runt of the personal-luxury litter.

The '67 was commonly judged a better all-around performer than its predecessor, but it retained the pillow-soft ride of earlier 'Birds. *Motor Trend* rated the '67 model a poor handler compared to any of the GM E-Bodies. On the other hand, Dearborn's entry rode better, particularly in pockmarked urban war zones, and stopped quicker with its standard front disc brakes than any of the General's troops.

	1966 Thunderbird	1967 Thunderbird
Base price	$4,395	$4,603
Price as tested	$6,010	$5,748
Engine	V-8, ohv	V-8, ohv

Bore x stroke	4.05 x 3.78 in.	4.13 x 3.98 in.
Displacement	390 cu. in.(1)	428 cu. in.(1)
Comp. ratio	10.5:1	10.5:1
Bhp @ rpm (gross)	315 @ 4,600	345 @ 4,600
Torque @ rpm (gross)	427 @ 2,800	462 @ 2,800
Carburetion	1 x 4 bbl	1 x 4 bbl
Final drive ratio	3.02:1	3.00:1
Steering		
Turns lock-to-lock	3.6	3.7
Turning circle	42.6 ft.	42 ft.
Brakes f/r	Disc/drum	Disc/drum
Construction	Unit-body	Perimeter frame
Front suspension	Independent, coil springs	Independent, coil springs
Rear suspension	Live axle, leaf springs	Live axle, coil springs
Tires	8.15 x 15	8.15 x 15
Wheelbase	113.0 in.	117.0 in.(2)
Overall length	205.4 in.	209.4 in.(2)
Overall width	77.3 in.	77.3 in.
Overall height (empty)	52.7 in	53.8 in.
Front track	61.0 in.	62.0 in.
Rear track	60.0 in.	62.0 in.
Curb weight	4,700 lb.	4,640 lb.(2)
Performance(3)		
0-60	11.4 sec	9.0 sec
1/4-mile	18.3 sec @ 77 mph	16.8 @ 86 mph
Braking, 60-0	157 ft.	143 ft.
Production	69,176	77,956

(1) The 428-c.i.d. engine was optional in '66, and the 390 still standard in '67.
(2) for four-door Landau tested. Two-door models measured 115 inches in wheelbase, 206.9 inches overall, weighed approximately 100 pounds less.
(3) from *Motor Trend*, '66 Landau tested March '66; '67 four-door Landau tested August 1967.

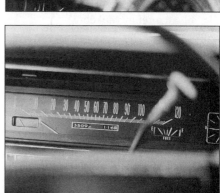

Facing page and left: Front-wheel drive allowed scads of foot and leg room, plus flat floors in both cars. **Below:** Rotating speedo is all part of the "brand new inside and out" styling and engineering philosophy bestowed on Toro. Cadillac's speedometer has conventional appearance and operation. **Bottom:** Toronado's fastback look contrasts strongly with Eldo's sculpted rear treatment.

I choose between them? I can't—and shouldn't. These are right-brain cars, cars that appeal to emotion over intellect, cars to stir the soul.

Which one stirs yours? ✍

Bibliography and Acknowledgments

Books: John A. Gunnell (editor) Standard Catalog of American Cars 1946-1975; *Maurice D. Hendry,* Cadillac, Standard of the World; *Jan P. Norbye and Jim Dunne,* Oldsmobile: The Postwar Years.

Periodicals: John R. Bond, "Oldsmobile Toronado," Road & Track, *November 1965; John Ethridge, "5 Luxury Specialty Cars,"* Motor Trend, *August 1967; Donald MacDonald and John Ethridge, various articles about Toronado,* Motor Trend, *December 1965; Robert Schilling, "Eldorado Switches From Push to Pull,"* Motor Trend, *January 1967; "Toronado,"* Motor Trend, *November 1965; "Olds Toronado,"* Car and Driver, *November 1965; "1967 New Car Buyer's Guide,"* Motor Trend, *November 1966; "Ford Thunderbird, Cadillac Eldorado,"* Car and Driver, *November 1966; "Cadillac Eldorado,"* Car Life, *April 1967.*

Thanks to GM designers Dave Holls, Chuck Jordan, and Stan Wilen; Kim M. Miller of the AACA Library and Research Center; Henry Siegle; and of course special thanks to current and former owners Jim Lemmon, Elbert Van Orden, and Dave Broadway.

Cadillac Clubs and Parts Suppliers

These clubs and resources listings were compiled in July 2000. For the most up-to-date information, consult the latest issue of *Hemmings' Vintage Auto Almanac* and the Hemmings web site at www.hemmings.com.

CLUBS

Allante Appreciation Group
P.O. Box 225
Edgewood, IL 62426
800-664-5224
E-mail: www.allante.org
Dues: $35/year
Membership: 1,650

Allante Owners' Association
140 Vintage Way, #146
Novato, CA 94945
888-ALLANTE
E-mail: allantefan@aol.com
Dues: $50/year
Membership: 2,500

Cadillac Club of North Jersey
20 Valley Ave. Ste D-2
Westwood, NJ 07675
201-263-0999
E-mail: www.tappedin.com/ccnj
Dues: $20/year
Membership: 275

Cadillac Drivers Club
5825 Vista Ave
Sacramento, CA 95824-1428
916-421-3193
Dues: $17.50/year
Membership: 120

Cadillac LaSalle Club Inc.
P.O. Box 1916
Lenoir, NC 28645-1916
828-757-9919
E-mail: www.cadlasal@twave.net
Dues: $30/year; Canada and Mexico: $40/year
Membership: 6,200

PARTS SUPPLIERS

Aabar's Cadillac and Lincoln Salvage and Parts
9700 NE 23rd
Oklahoma City, OK 73141
405-769-3318
E-mail: louannel@juno.com
Large source of comprehensive NOS parts and used cars for parts for 1939-1994 models

Dennis Ackerman
19 Gulf Rd.
P.O. Box 107
Sanbornton, NH 03269
800-487-3903
E-mail: dennis@caddyparts.com
Extensive selection of new and used parts for 1937-1976 models

Archive Replacement Parts
211 Cinnaminson Ave.
Palmyra, NJ 08065
609-786-0247
Stainless steel water outlet replacement for 1936-1948 Cadillac and LaSalle flat-head V-8 engines

CE Babcock
619 Waterside Way
Sarasota, FL 34242
941-349-4990
NOS and remanufactured sheet metal, chrome trim and stainless steel trim for 1941-1947 Cadillacs

Caddy Central
11117 Tippett Rd.
Clinton, MD 20735
301-234-0135
E-mail: cadlocator@aol.com
Bumpers and body parts for 1956-1970 Cadillacs

Cadillac King
9840 San Fernando Rd.
Pacoima, CA 91331
818-890-0621
E-mail: eldorado@gte.net
Large inventory of interior and exterior parts for 1950-1990 Cadillacs

Cadillac Parts and Cars Unlimited
46 Hardy Rd.
Sparks, NV 89431
775-826-8363
Reproduction exterior parts for 1938-1980 Cadillacs

Holcombe Cadillac Parts
2933 Century Ln.
Bensalem, PA 19020
215-245-4560
Fax: 215-633-9916
NOS, used and reproduction body trim, weatherstripping and air conditioning, brake and general mechanical and electrical parts for 1949-1983 Cadillacs

Honest John's Caddy Corner
P.O. Box 741
2271 FM 407 W
Justin, TX 76247
888-592-2339
E-mail: Honestjohn@website
Extensive line of new and used body parts for 1941-1991 Cadillacs

Piru Cads
402 Via Fustero Rd.
Box 227
Piru, CA 93040
805-521-1741
Large supply of body and trim parts for 1938-1953 Cadillacs

Sam Quinn Cadillac Parts
Box 837
Estacada, OR 97023
503-637-3852
Full line of engine parts for 1937-1977 Cadillacs

Dick Shappy Classic Cars
26 Katherine Ct.
Warwick, RI 02889
401-521-5333
Specializes in 1930-1933 V-16 parts

Robert H. Snyder
P.O. Drawer 821
Yonkers, NY 10702
914-476-8500
Extensive selection of original trim parts for 1941-1949 Cadillacs